THE   SONG

SONGBOOK "130"

Is a skillfully written compilation of over 130 Pop and R&B songs by music industry professional-songwriter and author, RICARDO A. WILSON.

Aspiring singers, songwriters, male and female can record these song lyrics in a studio recording session to any music production of their choice, to complete their demo album. Once these songs are mixed and mastered you then shop your project to independent and major record labels, with goals to secure a recording contract.

Ricardo Wilson has become one of the most highly sought after ghostwriters in Atlanta, Georgia. His timeless songwriting music lyrics' and style has been recognized and recorded by first time up and coming studio artist as well as multi-platinum Grammy award winning singers, song writers, and recording artist.

TABLE OF CONTENTS

1. BEAUTIFUL
2. SMILE
3. FEELING THE LOVE
4. FABULOUSNESS
5. SWEETEST VICTORY
6. LOVE HARD
7. SOARING EAGLE
8. TEAR DROPS
9. PEACEFUL JOURNEY
10. SHOULDER BAG
11. SCENTED PERFUME
12. CAN'T STAND YOU
13. STRIKING BEAUTY
14. THE LIMELIGHT
15. PARADISE
16. BREAK UP MUSIK
17. PILLOW TALK
18. MORE THAN FRIENDS
19. YOU GOT ISSUES
20. FAILED COMMITMENT
21. WAITING ON YOU
22. BLOWED AWAY
23. FROM HEAVEN
24. AWESOME
25. ALL I WANNA KNOW
26. SOME KINDA LUCK
27. CRIMINAL LOVE CHARGE
28. MOOD ON ZERO
29. THESE VOWS
30. APOLOGIZE
31. ON A MISSION
32. RISING SUN
33. LOVE OF THE ROSE
34. SEXY BODY
35. MISSING MY GIRLS
36. AN EMPTY SPACE
37. SCORNED
38. SO GLAD'
39. STALKIN'
40. HEELS AND LINGERIE
41. RIDING SOLO
42. BOY SHORTS

43. SPILLED MILK
44. TAKE CONTROL
45. GOOD AND WELL
46. SEX TAPE #2
47. IF YOU SAY SO
48. BE MINE
49.. FOUR WEEKS
50. THE RIGHT ONE
51. THE RIGHT ONE
52. TOLD YOU SO
53. A WIFE AND MISTRESS
54. A LITTLE BIRD
55. GREEN LIGHT
56. SLOW UP
57. BLUSH
58. IF I COULD
59. LOVE ENOUGH
60. MISERY LOVES IT
61. EXPENSIVE
62. CAT'S MEOW
63. CHEAPSKATE
64. NATURAL BEAUT
65. SO MAGNIFICENT
66. 80 REASONS
67. I AIN'T FINNA
68. THIS JOURNEY
69. SLEEPING WITH HER
70. FOOT FETISH
71. IN YOUR WORLD
72. YOUR GIRL
73. DREAM ABOUT YOU
74. BORN AND BRED
75. HIS LADY
76. SHAKE DOWN
77. SO CAN I
78. TEN TIMES
79. HAPPY DAYZ
80. HOLOGRAM
81. HITTIN' LIKE
82. NO MORE
83. THE SURPRIZE
84. WE GON' SHINE
85. FEAR NO THING

86. FIRST SITE
87. UP AT NIGHT
88. WE RALLY ON
89. IT'S BEST I LEAVE
90. I DON'T WANT HIM
91. WATCH
92. NO MORE KISSES
93. BIG MONEY
94. MOVE AND DIP
95. I CAN TELL
96. OUT MY WINDOW
97. BRO-KEN HEARTZ
98. FORBIDDEN WORD
99. MAKE MY BODY
100. LOVE SHOP
101. TRIALS AND TRIBULATIONS
102. BEHIND MY BACK
103. WATCH YOUR HOMEBOY
104. YOUR BABIES MOTHER
105. SWITCH SPEEDS
106. SOMEONE ELSE
107. DOCTOR
108. ON MY LAP
109. HOW COME
110. I LOVE THE STREETS
111. SOON OR A LATER
112. THIS LITTLE SPOT
113. MY COACH BAG
114. IN FOR THE NIGHT
115. SO SNEAKY
116. P.O.E
117. DADDY'S ANGEL
118. SLUMBER PARTY
119. A PARTY THIS WEEKEND
120. GIVING YOUR HEART BACK
121. LAST CALL
122. CHARM
123. HEY BARTENDER
124. HIGH SCORE
125. TO BE BOSS
126. WITH MY HEAD
127. DESIGNER SHADES
128. GIRL YOU'RE THE FINEST
129. GOT ME GOSSIPING
130. CHOCOLATE CAKE

[-] Quick Pause between words
[...] Long Pause between words
(1) Repeat

ALL SONGS WRITTEN, ARRANGED AND COMPILED BY
RICARDO A. WILSON. COPYRIGHT 2018.
PAIR THESE LYRICS WITH FREE INSTRUMENTALS ON YOUTUBE
THESE SONGS ARE TO BE RECORDED FOR PROMOTIONAL USE ONLY.
All RECORDINGS WILL RECOGNIZE THE AUTHOR FOR WRITING
CREDITS OR LICENSING OPTIONS.

MID TEMPO

BEAU-TI-FUL

INTRO:
      Life is so... Beautiful... So Beautiful...
Beau-ti-ful (beau-ti-ful)... beau-ti-ful...

BRIDGE:
      Cloud-nine-all-day-since-you been-a-way...
Smile-on-my-face when-I think-this way...
      I-can't-wait til fri-day (fri...day)....

VERSE I:
      Bless-ings from my girl...this is-how she-made-me...
      Ess-ence of bonjour-sprinkle it-by all means...
Who-would change-the world...
      Make it how it-should be..?
Dia-monds and-the pearls...
      Beau-ties more than skin-deep...

CHORUS: (REPEAT TWICE)

(1)

      You are so... Beau-ti-ful... so-(beau-ti-ful).
Beau-ti-ful (beau-ti-ful)... beau-ti-ful (beau-ti-ful)...
      Life is so... so-beau-ti-ful... beau-ti-ful...
Beau-ti-ful (beau-ti-ful)... (beau-ti-ful)...

VERSE II:
      Yes-ter-day-all day-and to-mor-row...
Se-ra-nade till-chills come-and eyes-close...
      Wish the-rain-go way-as the horns-blow...
Float-a-wa...y.

BRIDGE:

REPEAT CHORUS UNTIL MUSIC FADES OUT.

SLOW/MID TEMPO

SMILE

CHORUS:
      Make sure you smile... (it's a brighter day-Brighter).
      Real-big... smile... (keep your head up).
Make sure you smile... (at times-life gets hard but).
      Show-your..smile... chest out, head up. Make sure you smile.

VERSE I:
      Life-is just-so hard–sometimes–it... Breaks you-down...
      You're look-ing for- the strength- inside your- All burned-out...
      The bills-are due-you wan-na cry you... Don't stress-now...
      Dig-ni-ty and pride-arise-from no-where- Smile...

BRIDGE:
      Sel-fie day... flick a-way...   (2)
Ear to ear... smile for me too.
      Snap chat wave... A-O.K...
Facebook live...

MARY J. BLIGE TYPE SONG

CHORUS: (REPEAT TWICE)

VERSE II:
      I don't know-just where-this road-is go-ing... Round and-round.
      I'm search-ing for a-bett-er mo-ment... Like right... now.
      Po-verty and greed- they're clone-ing... No love found.
      You pave-the way-and then-you own-it... Your time now...

REPEAT BRIDGE AND CHORUS:

SLOW

FEELING THE LOVE

CHORUS:
        I'm... feel-ing... the love... the way... it goes.
I've... fall-en... in love... let it flow.
        I'm... feel-ing... the love... the way... it goes.
I've... fall-en... in love... love for sure.

VERSE I:
        So... outstanding... understand me (stand me)... BEAU-TI-FUL.
        Glow... so brightly... up inside me (side me)... you don't know.
        Cold... and tingling... flowing deeply (deeply)... lose control.
        No... I'm stingy... I ain't sharing (sharing)... so-lid gold.

(REPEAT CHORUS TWICE)

(3)

BEYONCE TYPE SONG

VERSE II:
        Whoa... to my baby... got me crazy (crazy)... mad mental.
        Float... till I'm flying... it's exciting (citing)... Geronimo.
        Show... like on Disney... am I dreaming? (dreaming?)... magical.
        No... one-eighty... three-sixty (sixty)... full circle.

BRIDGE: (REPEAT TWICE)
        I... love him so much... this feel is cra-zy.
I... love him so much yup... I love my ba-by.

REPEAT CHORUS UNTIL MUSIC FADES OUT.

POP

FABULOUSNESS

INTRO:
    I got the Fab-ulous.. (ulous)... (ness)(3).
I got the Fab-ulous... (ulous)...(ness)(3).

VERSE I:
    Detonate... the cute bomb, (cute bomb).
I'm the bomb.
    Pretty face... with no... flaws, (no flaws)
I'm a star.
    Can't regulate... sweetheart, (sweetheart).
Unless you God.
    Paper straight... a good job, (good job).
Don't work hard.
    Cartier... a nice charm, ice on.
On my arm.
    Chardonnay... a toast on, (toast on).
Being born...

GWEN STEFANI TYPE SONG

CHORUS: (REPEAT TWICE)
    I got the Fabulous... ulous... (ness)(3)
Excellence... and strength... no weak-ness, (ness)(3)
    I got the Fabulous... (ulous)... ness (3)
I'm all about... (about)... my busi-ness... (ness)3

VERSE II: **(4)**
    Better shape... unique huh? (unique huh?)
Perfect form.
    Let'em hate... and sleep on, sleep on.
Women scorned.
    Ride the wave... the beat on, (beat on).
That's my song.
    Everyday... can be fun, (be fun)
That's my song.
    Paper chase... a million, (million)
Mission on. Blessed the day... and preach on,
    (preach on). Reek's hit song.

REPEAT CHORUS UNTIL MUSIC FADES OUT

SWEETEST VICTORY

BRIDGE/INTRO:
      Nothing can hold me, (hold me), (hold me)...
Nothing can hold me, (hold me), (hold me).

VERSE I:
      When-you feel... me I'll-be there...
Gaining up on you, hear the cheers...
      Giving my all so be prepared...
Taking the lead, I'm almost, there...
      Climbing the highest atmosphere...
Pouring out blood, and sweat, and tears.
      Race to the top, the coast, is clear...
Fight to the fin-ish, have no fear.

FULL BRIDGE/PRE-HOOK: (5)
      Nothing can hold me... (hold me), (hold me)...
I won't fall back... the end... is near...
      Pain burning slowly... (slowly), (slowly)...
Smelling the triumph in the air...

                        KATY PERRY TYPE SONG

CHORUS:
      I'm gonna win the sweetest victory (1), victory (1), victory (1), victory.
      So I can finally place in history (1), history (1), history (1), history (1).
      Victory (victory). Victory (1), victory (1), victory
Never letting nothing-get to me (1), get to me (1), get to me (1), get to me (1).

VERSE II:
      I am the great-est none... com-pares...
Up for the cha-llenge... nev-er scared...
      Soar through the clouds... speed through... the air
I'll be the champ-ion, far-or near...
      Rip through the pain... as anguish clears...
Hurdle the mountains, climb like stairs...
      Pain is just weakness, leaving here...
I am a winner, hear... my cheers.

REPEAT CHORUS UNTIL MUSIC FADES OUT.

SLOW

LOVE HARD

VERSE I:
    The rain has settled down... sun came out...
Clear blue skies... butter-flies... (butter-flies)...
    Wearing my see through gown... thru the house...
Natural high... from last... night... (last-night)...

BRIDGE:
    I'm so scared... I don't wanna be alone... It's not fair...
    That you come and go home... Your kinds rare...
I can't have you for my own... I won't share...
    Cause these feelings won't go oh so.

CHROUS: **(6)**
    Will you love me..? I need you-to love me real hard...
    Will you love me..? I need you to love me real hard...
    Will you love me..? I need you to love me real hard.
        (6)
Will you love me..? (Will you love me?)
                                KERI HILSON TYPE SONG

VERSE II:
      A shot-without sound... knocks me down... blood shot eyes...
    Whiskey Lime... (whiskey lime).
      What am I feeling now..? Rubbing down... my spine-then to my
    Thy's... (my thys)...

REPEAT BRIDGE ONCE:

REPEAT CHORUS UNTIL MUSIC FADES OUT.

POP

SOARING EAGLE

VERSE I:

  Fly… like an angel… high… You can't stop-me anymore….
  Fear no danger… dashing night-gripping his sword…
  El-evator… ri-sing faster than before…
Now or never… pass the clouds… begin to soar.

BRIDGE:

  Go-ing… Go-ing… Stronger than before…
Go-ing… go-ing… Winning need for more…
  Endur-ing… endur-ing… Stronger than before…
Enduring… enduring… Winning need for more.

CHORUS: REPEAT TWICE

  Free… like the eagle soaring… glide… and forever going.
  Fly… like an Angel, (angel), angel.
 Free like an Eagle soaring… high and forever going…
  Fly… like the eagle… (I'm gonna take you high…er) and higher.

VERSE II:
      (7)
BRUNO MARS TYPE SONG
  Coast… as the wind blows… sun shine…
Peek-ing through the storm…
  Like a shuttle… leaving earth…
to the unknown…
  They won't break us… spread my wings…
I'm way to strong…
  Flying so free… it's a must… I carry on.

REPEAT CHORUS UNTIL MUSIC FADES OUT

POP

TEAR DROPS

VERSE I:

   Here we are... I smell'er perfume...
And she still crying... What am I gonna do...?
   She hurt's so bad... she's so confused....
Her dude stay trippin'... should I just play it cool..?
   We once had love... Now where just friends...
And I promised... to hold'er down till the end...
   He don't show love... It's on us now...
We head to the bedroom... she wants me to, take'er (down)...

CHORUS:

   Tear drops fallen... he keep calling...
Cause she ran off... she's with me... she been scarred...
   Tear drops fallen... she keep bawling...
She needs love ... Confessions of... A broken heart...

(8)

TORY LANEZ TYPE SONG

VERSE II:

   Hey sweetheart... he's looking for you...
Your I phones buzzing... what are you gonna do?
   Don't look sad... you're feeling abused...
I'll be ya' boyfriend... taking good care of you.
   He broke ya' love... it's okay now...
Let's head to the bedroom... So we can break it down.

BRIDGE:

   Out in... In out... Love in... She okay now...
Out in... In out... Love in... She okay now...

REPEAT CHORUS UNTIL MUSIC FADES OUT.

SLOW

PEACEFUL JOURNEY

VERSE I:
　　　　I can't go one day... not think-ing of you... (thinking of you) (1)...
　　　　The beauty of the after life is deja-vu.... (deja-vu) (1).
　　　　I had a cup of tea with ice... it went down smooth... (went down) (1)
　　　　Streaming on an astral flight-of sounds and tunes, (sounds and) (1).

BRIDGE:
　　　　Last-night I had a vision-strolling through the park we're chillin',
　　　　(chillin') (1).　joking bout the children, (children) (1).

CHORUS: (REPEAT TWICE)　　　　　　　　　　　　**(9)**
　　　　I'm wishing you a peaceful journey, (peaceful journey), peaceful journey, peaceful.
　　　　And I know you smile down on me, (smile down on me), smile down on me, smile down.
　　　　I'm wishing you a peaceful journey, (peaceful journey), peaceful journey, peaceful.
　　　　Soaring though the sky spread your wings, (sky spread your wings), sky spread your wings, sky spread.

VERSE II:
　　　　Whisper to myself... how much I miss you... (much I miss you) (1)
　　　　No one in the world could fit-in your shoes... (fit in your shoes)(1) Fit in your.
　　　　My tear dropped in the grass-and then-a rose... grew. (a rose grew), a rose.
　　　　I look up at the clouds the sky's-so blue, (so blue),

REPEAT CHORUS UNTIL MUSIC FADES OUT.

MID/UP TEMPO

SHOULDER BAG

VERSE I:
       You wanna show-that you like me, (like me)?
Then maybe you should just-buy-me-some-thing.
       You say my beauty make ya' heart speed,
(heart speed).
       Well c'mon big daddy and spend a-lil-mon-ey.
       A knock off purse won't excite me, ('cite me).
Not a Gucci from the discount swap meet.
       I know you long for a nice treat, (nice treat).
So get up off ya' butt and get-to-shop-ping.

BRIDGE:
       Get on up-and get to shopping... off ya' butt....
And buy me some-thing.
       Get on up-and get to shopping... off ya' butt...
And buy me something.

CHORUS: **(10)**
SZA TYPE SONG
       You gotta buy me a... (unh-unh) shoulder-bag (3)...
       A new leather... (unh-unh) shoulder bag (3).
I wanna see the... (unh-unh) brand new tag (3)...
       Cause I got class.
Where's my bag..? You need to buy me, (buy me), a
       lea-ther shoul-der bag (3).

VERSE II:
       I'm known to be a lil pricee (pricee)...
Cause this lovin' right here ain't-for-cheap...
       Louie, Gucci, or Brioni (Brioni)... I need
the finest leather on-my-bo-dy.
       I seen you pushin' that Bugatti (Bugatti)...
And the way ya' eyes ass-ault me.
       But before we leave the party (party).
You need to know what the deal is on me.

REPEAT CHORUS UNTIL MUSIC FADED OUT.

MID TEMPO

SCENTED PERFUME

VERSE I:

        I don't know... I couldn't say...
See it coulda' been... the other day...
        It mighta been... samples of sprays....
In a centerfold... magazine page...
        See what happened was... she had bumped into me.
Wait a minute nah... that happened yester-week.
        What I'm telling you... just slipped my memory.
I don't even know... will you stop quizzin' me, (cause).

CHORUS: (REPEAT TWICE)

        I... don't... know... why... I... smell... like... per-fume.
I... don't... know... why... I... smell... like... per-fume.
        It wasn't me... Ba-by pleaaase...
Down on my knees... Ba-by pleaaase...

TREY SONGS TYPE SONG

VERSE II:
        (11)
        As soon as I... enter your place...
You're looking for... rea-sons to blame...
        Constantly... searching for ways...
For an argument... pleadin' my case...
        Now based upon... throughout our history...
I usually... don't let you get to me...
        Late-ly... focused on other things...
I don't even know, why you're not trusting me (girl).

REPEAT CHORUS UNTIL MUSIC FADES OUT.

MID

CAN'T STAND YOU

CHORUS:
        I... can't... stand... you... since you left me lonely.
Running round-late night with your homies.
        Knowing you...hooked up with that girl. (girl)
I... can't... stand... you... Coming round acting phoney...
        Wish I... had a hammer on me... After I...
Gave you my whole world...

VERSE I:
        Better gone... gone get out my face... won't you...
Please just go away... hope you... have a real bad day... (Jackass)
        I sit at home... hopeing you're okay... when you... call
you always say... baby... that I'm on my way... (lies)
        Probably wrong... to hit you in the face... cause I'll...
may-be catch a case... sending the... police on a chase... (a chase)
        Every time... I for-give you-you take... take my kindness the wrong way... then it ends in a mistake.

REPEAT CHORUS TWICE:

(12)

VERSE II:
        SZA TYPE SONG
        On the phone... the thot den called my place... tryin'...
        hard to instigate... hope-ing... to feel me up with hate.
        Heart of stone... yup, that's just what you made... can't believe...
        that I use to say... that I loved you everyday...
        In a zone... hurt from all this pain... hate that... it had to...
        be this way... cause you chose to play this game.

STRIKING BEAUTY

VERSE I:
                As she moves a-long…
Been watch-ing her so long…
                Boy, she turns me on…
I want this la-dy…
                Emo-tions burn-ing strong…
Like my favorite song…
                The words go… how I want her
to have my baby.
                This is what-I want…
Bit-ten by-her love…
                Where my kiss-and hugs…
I can feel… al-ready…

CHORUS:
                She drives men-cra-zy…
She got that-spe…cial thing…   **(13)**
               She drives men cra-zy…
Drop dead-stri-king beau-ty…
                She drives men cazy…
Can't believe-what I am feel-ing…
                She drives men cra-zy…
I'll prob-ably buy-a-ring.

VERSE II:
                Damn my mind-is gone…
I'm fade-ing in a zone…
                Wishing I was home… alone…
with this la-dy…
                Dreaming all-day long…
How I'd make-her moan…
                Am I-feel-ing love…
or just-cra-zy…
                This is what-I want…
Bit-ten by her love…
                Where's my kiss-and hugs…
I can feel… al-ready.

THE LIME LIGHT

CHORUS:

      I wanna be in the... lime light... and movie screens...
      Bright lights-and V.I.P.... huge crowds... paparazzi flashing me...
      I wanna be in the... spot light-on t.v. screens...
Lifestyle your wildest dreams... in Hollywood... with stars...
      We're rich as can be... (can be), can be.

VERSE I:

      Glitz and glam-our huge smile on my face...
Cen-ter of att-ention right a-way...
      En-tour-age so deep we run the place...
And I-been dreaming- bout this life all day.

BRIDGE:

      I...can see myself... a star.... that's shining (2)...
Take... the world by storm... they all... like me (2)...
      I... can feel the joy... so en-ticing (2)...
Take... the world by storm... And liv-ing my dreams (2)...

REPEAT CHORUS TWICE

      (14)

TAYLOR SWIFT TYPE SONG

VERSE II:

      Bey-on-ce's dance moves on the stage (3)...
Mo-vie deals, en-dorse-ments on the way (3)...
      I know-I-work-hard-for-what it takes (3)...
I-want-it-so-bad... I just want a taste (3)...
      First class flights... and private jets today (3)
Fans-shake-my-hand-say-they're-glad-that I came...
      Cali-forn-ia, New-york, on my way (3)...
I-want-it-so-bad-I- just want a taste.

SLOW

PARADISE

VERSE I:

      You-know… I'm-in love with you… my life- ain't been-the same-since you…
      You're my heart… and precious jewel… so I wanna give the world to you…
      Like a yacht… that sails so smooth… or stroll the island sands… between our toes no shoes…
      Take a flight tonight… we so cool… in a world of love… and taboo.

CHORUS: REPEAT TWICE

      Pa-ra-dise… we-will find… in-due-time… you and I…
      Pa-ra-dise… Love-so blind… Life of pleas-sure… Settled in ya' mind…

VERSE II:

                                                           (15)

                             ELLA MAI TYPE SONG

      Let's swim… in the ocean blue… can-dle light… on a train for two…
      Dance-in close… As we play-the blues… holdin' hands… I'm in love-with you.
      Astral plane… what a mellow mood… guided by… the divine so true…
      I wanna take you there… my boo just sit back for the ride… let's just-cruise.

REPEAT CHORUS UNTIL MUSIC FADES OUT.

SLOW

BREAK UP MUZIK

VERSE I:

      I-been-goin' through it… I hear-it in my songs… Some-times-love is foolish… tell-me-what's go-ing on…
      So-hard-to keep it moving… cry-ing-all night long…
      Why do you always hurt me..? Why would you do me wrong..?
      Who's loving me… that's what you're won-der-ing…
      On-to-better things… I want us to end…. No suffering… I-will smile a-gain…
      Slow-song begin… and I'm listenin'.

CHORUS: (REPEAT TWICE)

      Break… up… muzik… break… up… muzik… Tears stop-flow-ing… love heals-slow-ly…
      Break… up… muzik… break… up… muzik… Pain… hurt… so… deep… bass… keep… ride-ing…

VERSE II:

                        (16)

      Bro-ken heart a-busein'… Pain-hurt leave me lon'…
      True love… Inde…pend…dent true-love… ca-rry on…
      So-lost… In my-music… heart-felt spoke-n poem…
      Dog-me… I ain't-stupid… I-keep standin' strong… I no longer plead… start-ing a brand new page…
      That's how it's gonna be… I-gotta pave the way… It took awhile to see… time-to make a change…
      This new part of me… seeing brighter days….

REPEAT CHORUS UNTIL MUSIC FADES OUT.

SLOW

PILLOW TALK

VERSE I:

        Lay your head-down on... my pillow...
Let me pull-your bo-dy... next to mine...
        As I lick-down to... your naval...
So your heart-rate and... my pleasure rise...
        Make you feel-the way... A wo-man should...
And you begin to think... it feels... so good...
        Now you can't hold back-the rest... it's time...
Shower to shower... My pillows shy. (She talkin' that)...

CHORUS: (REPEAT TWICE)

        Pill-ow talk... Pill-ow talk... she starts moanin' as we
move slow motion talkin'...
        Pill-ow talk... Pill-ow talk... lips start whisperin', chill
bumps fillin' in...

VERSE II:

(17)

        Pull the drapes-across... the window...
A little foreplay for the... midnight ride...
        Play the music slow... the tempo...
No more hurt and no more lies...
        Let me slowly lay your body down...
And you like the way I put it down...
        I can be-the what you often need...
Come and tell me where your secrets lead...

REPEAT CHORUS UNTIL MUSIC FADES OUT.

SLOW

MORE THAN FRIENDS

CHORUS:

        I wanna be more, (we should be more)…
I wanna be more, (we should be more)…
        More than friends (more than friends)…
I need to be more (we need to be more)…
        I need to be more, (if only we were)…
More than friends (more than friends)…

VERSE I:

        How long … will we play these games?
When I'm the one… that heals your heart… (broken heart)
        You lay… in my arms some days…
Crying tears-till we depart… (don't depart)…
        I don't know if I should say this…
Nor do I know-where I should start…
        I sacrifice our long lived friendship…
To be the one-you give your heart… (baby)…

REPEAT CHORUS TWICE:
        (18)

VERSE II:

        I feel… the pass-ion la-dy…
I wanna hug you like a scarf…
        One time almost kissed your lips…
The most beautiful, in the south…
        Don't hold back these feelings baby…
Place your hands here on my heart…
        I know they say that friends don't make it…
But they don't know how deep we are…

REPEAT CHORUS UNTIL MUSIC FADES OUT.

SLOW

YOU GOT ISSUES

INTRO/BRIDGE:

      You got some, (you got some)…
Is-sues boy, (is-sues boy)…
      Actin' all, (act-in' all)…
Pa-ra-noid, (pa-ra-noid)…

VERSE I:

      I don't wan-na be… trapped-in…
Your jea-lous-y… (boy)
      In-sec-ur-ities… cause-ing strain…
On you and me… (babe)
      I will ne-ver cheat… why you think the worst of-me… (boy)
      It's been drain-ing me… Be-cause I put my trust in we…

CHORUS: (REPEAT TWICE)

      These… lil' is-sues you-got…
They're going to bring-the worst-out of us…
      Ba-bay these… lil' is-sues must stop…
'Fore you make me run off (hey hey)

(19)

VERSE II:

      Why does it always seem… that you're check-ing-on me…? (hey)
      And you wan-na bring… up all kinda old-er things.
      You should trust in me like we put our trust in we…
      We were once a team now it seems to be a dream….

REPEAT CHORUS UNTIL MUSIC FADES OUT.

FAILED COMMITMENT

VERSE I:

Unhappily after all... but I'm so glad you called... I'm sorry he broke your heart... I told you that from the start...
Whenever you need to talk... I'll always play my part...
Shed some light when it's dark... Heal up all your wounds and scars.

BRIDGE:

You deserve a man-that's gonna love you. Complement and cherish all you do.
Happiness will always see you through. Don't worry there are plenty other dudes.

CHORUS: (REPEAT TWICE)

If I were you I'd leave... him... you don't... need him...
One-reason... because he won't commit...
You den' caught him cheatin'... he keep... schemin'... no
feelins'... plus he wont commit... (won't commit).

VERSE II:

(20)

He don't know how hard... for us to let down our guards...
Show'em how strong you are... cause you are not a part time broad.
Get in ya' fancy car... Drive till sunset super far... Cause he ain't gonna bend at all...

REPEAT BRIDGE ONCE

REPEAT CHORUS UNTIL MUSIC FADES OUT.

SLOW

WAITING ON YOU

VERSE I:

  Thinking bout you boy… you brighten up my day…
  Looking at my watch… It's about time-for you to walk my way…
  Like a kid with a new toy… you put a smile on my face…
  I can't hardly wait… cause I know one day you'll make a play…

CHORUS: (REPEAT TWICE)

  Wait…ing… on… you… Wait…ing… on … you… Pa…tient… for… you… to make your move… (to make your move)…
  Wait…ing… on… you… Wait…ing… on… you… Pa…tient… for… you… to make your move… (so make it smooth)

VERSE II:

  Whatchu gonna do boy..? Wishing like my birth-day…
  Cut into the chase-baby don't be shy… I'm sweet like chocolate cake… **(21)**
  I would like to enjoy… a warm evening… a dinner date…
  Will you take the bait..? 'Cause I'm nervous now… and trying not to wait…

BRIDGE: (REPEAT TWICE)

  I see you… you see-me… us together… Happ-ily…
  I see you… watching me… us together… Harmony…

REPEAT CHORUS UNTIL MUSIC FADES OUT.

MID/UP TEMPO

BLOWED AWAY

INTRO:
        She got'em blowed (blowed), away, (away)…
She got'em blowed (blowed) away, (away)…

VERSE I:

        What's up sexy… (hey) what's your name?
Dior complement your body, in a special way…
        Hey it's cool… let's cut to the chase…
I been seein' how you watchin' me-and I feel the same…
        Goin' down… ba-bay stare-in' at cha'.
Bo-d(a)y drive me cra-z(a)y.
        Music loud… lady… we should spend some time and start to dating.

people in the place…   **(22)**

CUTTY CARTEL LIKE SONG

CHORUS:
        When she walk up in the party, party
As she strut around they jockin'…
        See the looks on all their face.
She got'em blowed, (blowed)(2)-Away… (way)(2)
        Blowed, (blowed)(2)… Away… (way)(2).

VERSE II:
        You gon' love me… babe don't play no games…
Got the champagne in the bottles…dress to slay…
        Ain't no rules… I'm blowed away…
I'm already thinkin'… bout a wedding rang…
        Goin' down ba-bay… stare-in' atcha…
bo-d(a)y drive me cra-z(a)y.
        Music loud… lady… we should spend some time and start dating.

REPEAT CHORUS UNTIL MUSIC FADES OUT.

SLOW

FROM HEAVEN

VERSE I:

        The whole wide world is yours... (la-day).
Your gorgeous face I'm blown ... (a-way).
        God has given his An-gel... (wings).
And you're the fly-est in awhile I've... (seen).

BRIDGE:

        Beau-ty out-side... as well as-inside...
Beau-ty outside... as well as-inside...
        Girl you so-fine... one of-a kind...
Girl you-so fine... one of-a kind...

CHORUS: (REPEAT TWICE)

        I ain't never seen... you out in them streets...
Gorgeous in the world... your shape is so mean...
        Beauty of a queen... any rich man's dream...
Gotta be... must be... from heaven.

(23)

                            MIQUEL TYPE SONG

VERSE II:

        I just wan-na know your (name).
You got me high like nova-(cane.)
        Where you come from..? Where you stay?
Must be from a spe-cial place..?

BRIDGE:

REPEAT CHORUS UNTIL MUSIC FADES OUT.

MID

AWESOME

CHORUS:

      I'm good I'm feeling awe-some…
I'm good good I'm feeling awesome…
      Soaring over king-dom come…
Baby ya' love-take my heart-away…

VERSE I:

      You give me-a reason… to wear a smiling face…
You fill an empty space… you're… my heart…
      You're keeping me chee-zing… my heart begin to race…
Chills run through my frame… a love… scar…

BRIDGE: (24)

      I don't need no other (other)…
Your all that I need (need)… (all that I need).
      Others lost in wonder…But you
cat-er to me… (you cater to me).

REPEAT CHORUS TWICE:

ALICIA KEYS TYPE SONG

VERSE II:

      If love was-a sea-son… we'd make it everyday…
A ro-man-tic escape… or at-our… home…
      Learn-ing and teach-ing… to love in certain ways…
So good I'm fiending … so I have-to say.

BRIDGE:

REPEAT CHORUS UNTIL MUSIC FADES OUT.

SLOW

<u>*ALL I WANNA KNOW*</u>

VERSE I:
   Been ten-whole days…
It's kind-a strange…
   And she won't stay…
Why-things have changed…
   Am-I the blame…
Cause I-am in pain…
   I fill my brain…
With pur-ple rain…

BRIDGE/PREHOOK:
   She won't an-swer her phone…
Record-ing coming on…
   she won't pick-up her phone… **(25)**
Voice mail-keep com-ing on…

<u>*TANK TYPE SONG*</u>

CHORUS:
   All I wanna know (all I wanna know),
All I wanna know (all I wanna know)…
   Are you-breaking up-with me? (breaking up with me?)
Breaking up with me? (breaking up with me)..?
   How you gonna go, (how you gonna go)….
How you gonna go, (how you gonna go)…
   And play me ba-by, (play me ba-by)…
Play me ba-by, (play me ba-by)..?

VERSE II:
   It's not o-kay…
Your cheat-ing ways…
   And it's a-shame…
You-play these games…
   Tell me-his name…
Is he-your mane..?
   You let him bang..?
Are-you insane…? (hey)…

BRIDGE/PREHOOK REPEAT UNTIL MUSIC FADES OUT.

SLOW

SOME KINDA LUCK

VERSE I:

        All I know… is I'm-thank-ful…
My heart… and soul-she so-spe-cial…
        We… have chose… to seize the role…
on the beau-ti-ful… side… of a mir-a-cle…
        And she loves me… Love cri-ti-cal…
We're so emo-tion-al… who love who the most?
        And stunning… gorgeous to the bone…
Keep her… pic-ture on… my new I-phone…

CHORUS: (REPEAT TWICE)

        I'm so lu-cky… like three wish-es…
or a prince-the princess kiss-es…
        Like a clover… that's been missin'…
I'm so lu-cky… you're my wo-man…

VERSE II:
        (26)

        Girl I chose… the per-fect rose…
Im-poss-i-ble… like the four leaf-clove…
        Time has shown… we in-sep-erable…
Un-deni-able… cause' we're so close…
        And my dear… she put on a show…
All de-signer clothes… just-to let you know…
        So be clear… we can on-ly grow…
In the bed-we-hold…with our eyes closed.

REPEAT CHORUS UNTIL MUSIC FADES OUT.

MID

CRIMINAL LOVE CHARGE

VERSE I:

      Cu-pid shot me... In love with a-thief...
May sound cra-zy... cause my ba-by... he just robbed me...
      Where's the po-lice...? cause we in high-speed...
On a chase... play-in kissy face... deep-in love we...
      I cannot breathe... reg-ular-ly... all my love...
for you babe... deep in love we...
      So exciting... Cl-yde and Bon-nie... warm embrace...
      for the take... hands-up-I freeze.

CHORUS: (REPEAT TWICE)

      Cri-mi-nal... love... cha-rge... He stole-my....
heart... and can't be-caught...
      Crim-mi-nal... love... charge... love-in so...
good... I swear he need to catch a charge...

VERSE II: (27)

      Con-spi-rac-cy... cause we a team... love my
ba-by, dan-ger-ously... like I'm a fiend...
      I am his queen... he is my king... us a-gainst...
the universe huh...? Everything green... How he has me..?
      It's a rob-bery...in a trance... We start dancing...
and roman-cing... it's a story... love and glory... it is one of the
      wildest sto-ries... con-vict-ing... me...

REPEAT CHORUS UNTIL THE MUSIC FADES OUT.

SLOW

MOOD ON ZERO

VERSE I:

        Torn-a-part… love-been-lost…
cry-in… foun-tain… bro-ken heart-ed…
        Scorn-and-scarred… ta-ken hard…
Frown-and pout-in… try-na fight-it…
        How-you-do-in? Down-and-blue-in…
Who-you-fool-in… I'm gon-na get through-it…

CHORUS:

        I ain't even in the mood…
Cause my mo-od on… mood on zero…
        I ain't even in the mood…
Cause I'm torn up, (yup) I'm torn up…
        I ain't even in the mood…
Cause my mood… mood on zero…
        Wounded heart, I'm feel-n rude…
Cupid choked up… and he then lost love… (oh)!

VERSE II:

        (28)

        Stroll-the-park… af-ter dark… hurt
been heightened… and I been cry-n…
        Notes and cards… ripp-ed a-part…
Pic-ture burn-in… ease-the-mo-ment…
        So abused… play-ed the fool…
Emo-tions cloud-ed… try-na fight it…

REPEAT CHORUS UNTIL MUSIC FADES OUT.

SLOW

THESE VOWS

VERSE I:

        I saw doves... remembering when we... met...
E-ter-nal love... tak-ing a-way my... breath...
        Speak these words... flowin' thru my chest...
One-found love... the mo-ment never left...

BRIDGE:

        Will you take these vows and... love me
'til the end of... time...
        I'ma say these vows and... love you...
will you be my wife..?

CHORUS: REPEAT TWICE

        Our life's like a love song... I know, I know, I know...
She's what makes my heartbeat... Hello, hello, hello...
        There could be no o-ther... oh no... oh no... oh no...
Everyday and all week... All day, all day, all day...

VERSE II: (29)

        Take this ring... the finger on the left...
A choir sings... our parents to the left...
        A precious queen... The king's heart check...
Everything... you want-I wanna get...

BRIDGE:

REPEAT CHORUS UNTIL MUSIC FADES OUT.

SLOW

APOLOGIZE

VERSE I:

       Ba-by plead... plead to me... cause you and I both know...
It's been an uphill ba-ttle...
       Leave ya' keys... Don't talk to me... unless... you... apologize, (apologize)....
       I can't understand boy...
Why you don't wan-na be here?
       Sometimes ya' words get so cold...
It's hard for me to be here...

CHORUS: (REPEAT TWICE)

       Why don't you apo-lo-gize..?
Attitude's from you is unfair...
       Why don't you apo-lo-gize..?
Let's work it out and make things more clear...

(30)

VERSE II:

       Is this the end..? I gave my all for sure...
tonic and gin... get's me through the storm...
       Cer-tain things... you say to hurt no more...
bags are by the door... I won't ask no more...

REPEAT CHORUS UNTIL MUSIC FADES OUT.

MID

ON A MISSION

VERSE I:

        Mar-vin Gaye and Char-donnay... and a few other things is al I need...
        To show how much I appreciate...
The joy and the smile-you bring to me...
        Can't ex-plain the feelings that...
often covers over me...
        All I know, when I'm with you...
Heaven flows in harmony...

CHORUS: (REPEAT TWICE)

        I'm on a mis-sion... to love ya'...
Heart-rate tellin' me hurry up...
        I'm on a mis-sion... to love ya'...
I can't stop or get enough...

VERSE II:

(31)

        On my life on everything... You truly mean the world to me...
        Traveling on this lone-ly road...
leading to you next to me...
        I'll walk across the promise land...
searching for our ecstacy...
        If you're lost in afterlife...
I'll search for an eternity...

REPEAT CHORUS UNTIL MUSIC FADES OUT.

SLOW

RISING SUN

CHORUS:

       Rise... rise... rise... (We rise with-the sun)...
Rise... rise... rise... rise... (We rise with the sun)...
       Rise... rise... rise... rise... (We rise with the sun)...
Rise... rise... rise... (We rise with the sun)...

VERSE I:

       Ma-king love all night-we've just begun...
You and I-with no clothes-we're one on one...
       Flow-ing seas-as the ocean's deep,
And the feelings there, oh! The feel-ings there.
       See myself in your eyes-and I am sprung...
Your bo-dy's calling for mines-here I come...
       Need you here in my life to love and
don't go no where-and just stay until we...

REPEAT CHORUS: ADELE TYPE SONG

       (32)

VERSE II:

       Can-dle light on-ly right the wax still burn...
Kiss my neck-and my chest-favor returned...
       Mes-merized as I roll my eyes...
Lost up in his spell-like a fairy tale...
       I'm in love, my heart weighs a hundred tons...
Hear the bird's that's in love-I know this song...
       Don't go no where-day breaks near, and just stay
right there, you just stay right there, we...

REPEAT CHORUS UNTIL MUSIC FADES OUT.

SLOW

LOVE OF THE ROSE

VERSE I:

        I just wan-na give… my heart…
Only if… you want… it babe…
        I've been love-ing from… the start…
I hope you do more than-feel me… (feel me)
        Huffin', puffin' in the dark…
Whisper low… say my name…
        Feel so good to be a part…
of ya' world sexy babe…

CHORUS: (REPEAT TWICE)

        Love me like the love… of the rose…
Love me like the thought… of the rose…
        Love me like the scent… of the rose…
Love me like the rose… the rose…

VERSE II:

(33)

        Take me to a per-fect place…
Perfect like the month… of May…
        Tell me every single day…
That you love me… (that you love me)…
        I cherish every word you say…
Make believe the stars…fall…
        Make a wish from which… it stands…
ba-bay… al-ways… ba-bay…

REPEAT CHORUS UNTIL MUSIC FADES OUT.

MID TEMPO
SEXY BODY

CHORUS:

       Girl you got a sex-y bo-dy...
I just wanna dance with you...
       Damn, you got a sex-y bo-dy...
I just wanna hold ya' hips... and move like this...

VERSE I:

       If beauty was a shining star...
It sparkles cause how fine you are...
       Your glow can light a sky that's dark...
I hope that I can shine with you...
       You're the one that turns me on...
All the others blow right by me...
       In the club-make this our song...
I just want you pressed besides me...

REPEAT CHORUS TWICE

VERSE II:

(34)

       You got me look-ing so damn hard...
Got me kinda-off my guard...
       You killin'em-need be behind bars...
Hands down-the flyest in the party...
       You got the perfect skin tone...
I wanna rock with you all night long.
       Fitted jeans... showing thong...
A private dance. That's what I want.

REPEAT CHORUS UNTIL MUSIC FADES OUT.

MID

MISSING MY GIRLS

VERSE I:

        I'm push-ing my caddi…
Fine and dandy… won-derful…
        Until I start missing home…
My life is cavi… I'm thankful gladly…
        Cause I know… life could be miserable…
Talk to my daddy… tell that I'm sadly… put-ting on…
        Tired of being all alone…
Homie sick badly… gotta make more cheese…
        eyes are closed… now I start to picture home…

CHORUS:

        I wanna kick it with my girl-friends…
I miss chillin' with my girl-friends…
        Reminisce when we were in school…
We were so cool… fun till the day ends…
        I wanna kick it with my girl-friends…
I miss chillin' with my girl-friends…
        Everyday I-constantly move…boy I
tell you, it ain't like it use to… (be).

VERSE II:
        (35)
        I gotta keep stea-dy…
Sometimes I'm ready… to hit the road…
        And go right back home…
I'm hugging my te-ddy… before I go bed-dy…
        bye-be gone… I'm all a-lone…
Up till the break of dawn… Member when Tam-my
        kissed Simone?
Club 112 is gone… falcons home's … Mercedes dome…

REPEAT CHORUS UNTIL MUSIC FADES OUT.

MID

AN EMPTY SPACE

VERSE I:
    I… don't wan-na be alone…
Nor-go out-on my own…
    No feel-ing inside, need you in my life…
I'm supposed to be so strong…
    It's hard to carry on…
No feel-ing inside… it's empty inside…

BRIDGE:
    I'm… so proud to be…
your shoulder piece…
    And I'm so glad, I found you…
Don't wanna live without you…
    I've been through things…
Some hurtful scenes…
    I'm good to go…
So you should know…

              (36)

CHORUS:
    You… cured a heart-break…
Wiped my tears-away…
    Made a brand new place…
You filled an em-pty space…
    You… cured a heart-break…
I'm so proud-to say…
    that you made a way…
You filled an empty space…

VERSE II:
    You… own the key… and the ring…
To how I act a-round you…
    My love is gon-na drown you…
Between the sheets… you comfort me…
    I'm good to go… you should know…

MID TEMPO

SCORNED

VERSE I:

        You-wanna leave... I wish you stay...
I miss-you babe... babe.
        He-took ya' heart, can't be replaced...
Thrown away... a-way...
        I give my all, and you won't change...
It's a shame... a shame...
        Down on my knees, you make me beg...
One leg... leg...

CHORUS: (REPEAT TWICE)

        He-scorned... her heart...
(He scorned-her heart)
        She-trust... no one...
(She trust-no one)
        He-scorned... her heart...
(He scorned her heart)
        Hell... hath no fu-ry...
Like a-wo...man's scorn...

                                                                  (37)

VERSE II:

        She has a heart, that's filled with [pain...
Whose to blame..? (blame..?)
        Way... deep inside... she's in my veins...
Co-caine... (caine...)
        She's like a drug, one hit you change...
A flame... (a flame...)
        Pride... broke-n-shame... her name...
Insane... (insane...)

REPEAT CHORUS UNTIL MUSIC FADES OUT.

SLOW

SO GLAD

CHORUS:

        I'm so... glad... that one-day... I met you...
I'm so... glad... from day-one we stayed true...
        I'm so... glad... our whole life-has been cool...
I'm so... glad... to say... that I- love you...

VERSE I:

        You-and I a-lone... lay-ing face to face...
Turn off-all the phones... lov-ing strong embrace...
        lon-liness is gone... grab you by the waist...
Proud to be your girl... there's no other way...

BRIDGE:

        Remind me of a movie... when Prince Charming's
kisses moved-me...
        Chills-running thru me... cause that's how real love should be...

REPEAT CHORUS TWICE:

        (38)

VERSE II:
        I want you to know...
I'm cra-zy for you babe...
        Love feeling so strong...
will never go away...
        Cu-pid made a day...
we love every day...
        Happi-ness for sure...
Forever and always...

BRIDGE:

REPEAT CHORUS UNTIL MUSIC FADES OUT.

UP TEMPO

STALKIN'

VERSE I:

        You know… you got me actin' cra-zy boy…
We feel-in love deep… so what-my heart-hurt for..?
        You know… you put-it on-me boy…
Your spell-is on me… why you wan-na leave-me for..?

BRIDGE:

        I know… your girl is phoney…
I'm sure… she ain't the real McCoy…
        I saw… you and her clubbing…
And followed you-right out the door…

CHORUS:

        He… got… me… stalk-in him…
(Stalk-in, stalk-in)
        Ask-in his boys… where he been…
And they say… they don't know…
        He-got-me… stalk-in him…
(Stalk-in, stalk-in)
        I feel… so rot-ten…
But I gotta have… some more-of him…

JASMIN SULLIVAN TYPE SONG

VERSE II: (39)

        Late… one night…I popped up on the scene…
When I pulled-up… I see a pink s.u.v..
        I called ya' cell phone… you lied to me…
Hopped out my car… and spray painted your SUV…
        (He got me stalk-in)

BRIDGE:

REPEAT CHORUS UNTIL MUSIC FADES OUT.

SLOW

HEELS AND LINGERIE

CHORUS:

        She in high... heels-and lingerie...
Today gotta be-my luck-y day...
        She in high... heels-and lin-ger-ie...
Sex-ie with a pre-tty face...

VERSE I:

        Stare-ing past the win-dow I...
Watch-as the cars ride by...
        Strutting cross the room she-fine...
Beau-ty she caught my eyes...
        Move-past the can-dle light...
Light-shine... on her thighs...
        Ba-by keep me in surprise...
Tak-ing the cake each time...

CHORUS: (REPEAT TWICE)

(40)

VERSE II:
        Meet me at my bed and climb...
On top of me and take your time...
        Ready for the bump and grind...
Sexy look-in your eyes...
        Ba-by girl she blow my mind...
Knock me off my feet-no crime...

BRIDGE/PREHOOK

        I want you... to leave them things on...
While we do... our thang-and freak on...
        I want you... to leave them things on...
While we do the do... and get our freak on...

REPEAT CHORUS UNTIL MUSIC FADES OUT.

MID

RIDING SOLO

VERSE I:
      I use to be the one-sitting at home… wait-in' on him…'til family comes home….
      I wouldn't believe this could happen to me.
I heard you whispering on your cell phone… If I pop your head… I'd be dead wrong…
      Poor little guy-think I can't see…
You come home-smell-in' like her perfume… leave a
      scent trail to the rest room. Little ol' me being naïve…

CHORUS:
      Chapt-er closed… we den' broke up-I'm moving on…
      I'm ridin' solo… (I'm ridin' solo). Hurt-no more…
close the book up-this chapter closed…
      I'm ridin' solo… (I'm ridin' solo)
Move-in on… we den broke up-that's how it goes…
      I'm ridin' solo… (I'm ridin' solo).
Feelings numb… use to tear up-but now I'm done…
      I'm ridin' solo… (I'm ridin' solo)

VERSE II:
      I spent many nights… listening to slow jams…fighting back
the tears-wondering what's wrong…. chillin' at the pad…
      while my man creeps… finally got the nerve… to stand
out on my own… face-in all my fears… and kept my heart strong…
      learning sacrifice- some treat-love cheap…
We are done… cause lately you been shade-ie…
      Number one, learn how to treat a lady…
We are done… I won't turn back-no ba-by…
      Here I come… to a new life… bet-ter appreciate me.

REPEAT CHORUS UNTIL THE MUSIC FADES OUT.

MID

BOY SHORTS

VERSE I:

      Ah look at me... dressed so clean I got to strike a pose...(Pose-I suppose)...
      Do you see... what I see-I'm comfortable don't need a slip or robe...(Robe-I suppose)...
      When I settle down... I think of you... The way you watch the way I move...
      Bring a smile-that stretch across my face.. I love the way... (I love the way-he say)

CHORUS: REPEAT TWICE

      He said he likes when I walk around in my (boy shorts).
      The top is matching I'm confortable in my (boy shorts).
      Oiled down I'm so sexy up in my (boy shorts). He on his way I must hurry put on my (boy shorts).

                            KERI HILSON TYPE SONG

VERSE II: (42)

      (Ooh)-seductively-passion waits and then we start to moan... (moan-I suppose)
      Submissively-pedals trail the room picked from a rose...
      (Rose-I suppose) Ba-by talk that talk, it's all for you...Sexy calves in my house shoe Just to please you-grab me by the waist. Then whisper when you say...

REPEAT CHORUS UNTIL MUSIC FADES OUT.

MID/COUNTRY

SPILLED MILK

VERSE I:

      I ain't worried bout-the past…
I'm pickin'up the broken glass…
      Can't miss the love we never had…
I moved on… I moved on…
      Don't explain cause I ain't mad…
Refuse to be all hurt and sad…
      You're lucky I ain't actin' a ass…
I'm not sweatin' o-va… I ain't sweatin' o-va…

CHORUS: REPEAT TWICE

      Spilled, (spilled)-milk, (milk)…
Ain't no need fa' cryin' no..
      Don't need to be cryin' ova…
Spilled, (spilled)-milk, (milk)…
      I'm okay irregardless so it
ain't no need to lyin' ova…

                    CARRIE UNDERWOOD TYPE SONG

VERSE II: **(43)**

      I knew that we were mov-ing fast…
A lot of things forgot to ask…
      Like one day when I thought you had…
A ring on… a ring on…
      I just found out about your dad…
You never took me to your pad…
      You know what though, I'm kinda glad…
It's O.V. I ain't sweatin' (I ain't sweatin')

REPEAT CHORUS UNTIL MUSIC FADES OUT.

MID

TAKE CONTROL

CHORUS:
        Take-control-of-me… Like I wanna be…
Take-control-of-me… I want you-to lead…
        Take-control-of-me… like-it-spose-to be…
Take-contol-of-me…Pour ya' love on me…

VERSE I:
        We can do it with the lights out… (lights out)
Or do you like it with the lights on…? (lights on?)
        Show me how to come the long route… (long route).
        Make me wanna take the short road… (short road).
        Lay my body down all night… (all night)
Rub me down fast or slow, (or slow)
        Come on baby don't be shy, (be shy)
Show me how deep that you can go…

REPEAT CHORUS (TWICE)   *RHIANNA TYPE SONG*

VERSE II: (44)
        I wonder can you get the grand prize..? (grand prize)? Can work it like I'm on a strip pole, (strip pole)
        I see you lookin' at my thick thighs, (thick thighs)
Put your hands right here and grip those… (grip thoughs)
        Ya' shoes lookin' like the right size, (right size)
For you I'm gonna give the best show, (best show)
        I'm tired of messin' with the nice guys, (nice guys)
I'm addicted to the bad and bold…

BRIDGE/PREHOOK:
        Baby give me that Her-cules…
Baby give me that, what I need.
        Baby give me that en-ergy…
Baby show me you're all that I need.

REPEAT CHORUS UNTIL MUSIC FADES OUT.

SLOW

GOOD AND WELL

VERSE I:
        Now I... can't think of a reason...
For me... to just-pack up and leave...
        You see... my heart-only bleed-and...
bump it's beat for you...
        And I... don't know what you are think-ing...
I love... you way too much... to play you... for the fool.

CHORUS:
        You know... good and well...
That I will never leave you... girl I really need you (1).
        You know... good and well...
I can't take another lost... another lost.
        You know... good and well...
All the things we been through... arguments we been through.
        You know... good and well... we stay to gether at all costs.

VERSE II: (45)

JAIMEE FOXX TYPE SONG
        You cried... and told me how you felt-and...
which lead to sus-picion of catching me cheating...
        The thing... I doubt that your see-ing my loyalty to you.
        Girl... I'm to real for schem-ing
And fake emotional mis-lead-ings...
        in time...you're goona kill the demons...
cause I... will not quit on you...

REPEAT CHORUS UNTIL MUSIC FADES OUT.

MID TEMPO

SEX TAPE #2

VERSE I:

        Tonight gon' be a freak show…
Like one-you never seen be-fore…
        We bought to get real down low…
Me and my girl gon get real nas-ty…
        First we gonna do it real slow…
Because she want a new lead role…
        My baby girl real thick so…
You're bout to see some real good act-ion…

CHORUS:

        She wanna do a new sex tape, (sex tape)
And I can't hardly wait…
        She wanna do a new sex tape…
This time-she wanna show her face…
        She wanna do a new sex tape, (sex tape)
She tryna' go to the bank…
        She wanna do a huge sex tape, (sex tape)
This time she gonna leak the tape.

VERSE II:

        (46)

        We got the lense to close…
We back it up and film some more…
        A script that has never been wrote…
She kinda wild scratching and biting.
        Her sexy ass bad though…
Smokin' like loud yo…
        This girl could never be broke…
If the internet know like I know…

REPEAT CHORUS UNTIL MUSIC FADES OUT.

SLOW

IF YOU SAY SO

VERSE I:
        I don't under-stand you…
You must don't under-stand me…
        because the way you think…
Always leave me crying…
        I swear… I gave all my love –in…
And thought they we were a pair…
        but you say that we wasn't…
so now to me its clear…
        Thanks to you for nothing…
I wiped away my tears…
        Excuse me-you say something..?
Go in and out my ears…

CHORUS: (REPEAT TWICE)

        If you… say so… all I know…
Been down-this road… but not-no more…
        If you… say so… packed my clothes…
Cause her you chose… but my heart broke…
        (If you… say so…)

VERSE I: (47)
        I thought-you were cool…
They say a dreamer stay sleep…
        Catch me lord before…
I'm fall-ing way to deep…
        I swear I gave all my love…
Thought we were a perfect pair…
        But you say you wasn't ready…
So now to me it's clear…
        Thanks to you for nothing…
I wiped away my tears…
        Excuse me you say something…
Go in and out my ears…

REPEAT CHORUS UNTIL THE MUSIC FADES OUT.

MID/UP TEMPO

BE MINE

CHORUS:

      I want you-to be mine... ba-by be my...
Valentine, (be my valentine)...
      Feel-ing special all night... celebrat-ing...
Valentine, (it's valentine's)
      Tree hundred six-five... celebrat-ing...
All the time... I want it all the time...

VERSE I:

      Give me some-thing good...
Give me something sweet...
      Like the melody we hear...
Flowing through the beat...
      Is that d.o.z.e.n.... just for me..?
The ex-pression of the rose-say l.o.v.e.e...
      Truly yours to keep...
Chocolate we can eat...
      As long as I am here with you...
Happy as can be...

REPEAT CHORUS TWICE:

(48)
BRIAN MCKNIGHT TYPE SONG

VERSE II:

      I will be your teddy bear...
You can be my candy...
      The love of cupid in the air...
Is all fine and dandy...
      Always know I'll be...
February 14th...
      And through all the day's of years...
I love you... You're my queen...

REPEAT CHORUS UNTIL MUSIC FADES OUT.

SLOW

FOUR WEEKS

CHORUS:
                Making love to her slow-ly…
And I be goin' so-deep…
                Give it to her so-good…
That she'll be sleep for four weeks…
                Making love to her slowly…
And I be going so-deep…
                Got her feel-ing so good…
That she'll be sleep for four weeks…

VERSE I: **(49)**

                World-renouned… break it down…
Love when you… make that sound…
                I got the best-sex in town…
Pound for pound… wear the crown…
                Swim well never drown…
Stroking round for miles…
                Pre-tty brown… wet and wild…
Go on and lift… up your gown…
                Cause I'm about to put it down…
Gorgeous smile… Hold it down…
                Hold it down, bang it out…

REPEAT CHORUS (TWICE):

VERSE II:
                Boo-ty round… moan-ing loud…
We sweat-ing, we don't need a towel…(beat it down)
            … in the house… on the couch…
On the ground… we mak-ing love… all a round…
                Sexy frown… steady now… for a-while…
She say she loving how I put it down…
                Pitchers mound… swing-hit wild…
In the clouds… she call it hea-ven now…

SLOW

THE RIGHT ONE

VERSE I:

And... I... been fiendin' all-day... just like-a bouquet... the catch of the day... is you babe...
I'm gonna need a lil change... I'm break-ing the bank... so is it o-kay... if you stay...
Now... let's cut to the chase... the VIP is the place... where we can take... some privacy babe...
Girl-your body and face... and this champagne... Tell-ing my brain... you're the one... (you're the one...)

CHORUS: (REPEAT TWICE)

Eani, meani, mynee, mo... you the baddest on the pole...
Wonder can I keep you tho... can I keep ya', (can I keep ya')...
Eani, meani, mynee, mo... you the baddest on te pole...
Should I keep'er, (should I keep'er)...?

VERSE II:

(50)

Come closer... drop it and shake...
Slow down the pace...Make me wait... (I like that...)
Who, who do I blame..? Because it's ashame... How perfect your shape... God gave his grace... I mean that...
Tell, (tell) me your name... Let's play a game... Fortune and fame... I got that...
Hey... you blow me away... I want you always... Selfish all day... Can I keep that?

REPEAT CHORUS UNTIL MUSIC FADES OUT.

SLOW

HOW YOU BEEN

VERSE I:

   We share... A bond... In between us...
Bind-ed by both of our hearts...
   I-can name... one million rea-sons...
Why... we should never de-part...

BRIDGE:

   You... have-my... un-di-vide-ed....
Love... on... de-mand...
   Been... search-ing... For a love like yours...
A-cross the land...

CHORUS: (51)
   Ba-by... how you been..? I miss-you...
And your love-in...
   Ba-by... where you been..? I saw your girls...
told them I love you...
   Ba-by... how you been..? I miss you dearly...
and your love-in...
   Ba-by... where you been...? I just want to say
I love you...

VERSE II:

   Your-job keep you leav-ing...
Keep-ing you is so hard...
   We hook up certain eve-nings...
I wish our time would never part...

BRIDGE:

REPEAT CHORUS UNTIL MUSIC FADES OUT.

TOLD YOU SO

VERSE I:

        I-had heard… he dated some-one…
Sex was good… said this some-one…
        When he's done… hav-ing his fun…
He moves on… to a-no-tha…

BRIDGE:

        You're my girl… we go way back…
Like straighten combs… and stock-ing caps…
        Al-ways know… I got your back…
For any-thing… Best to know that-but…

CHORUS: (REPEAT TWICE)   (52)

        I told you… I told you… I told you…
He was gon-na cheat… He was gon-na cheat…
        I told you… I told you… I told you…
Told you… you should leave… but you wasn't tryna hear
        It.

VERSE II:

        I know it hurts… I'm here to lean on…
Can't say why… on you… he could cheat on you?
        All them lies… for no rea-son…
Don't you cry… jus go and leave him…

BRIDGE:

REPEAT CHORUS UNTIL MUSIC FADES OUT.

MID

WIFE AND MISTRESS

VERSE I:

        I-got... a wife at home... and I love her...
My girl-friend... keep call-ing my phone... I can't answer...
        I know... what I'm doing wrong... growing
faster... Our love... is super duper strong... both lov-ers.

BRIDGE/PREHOOK:

        Torn between the two... tell-ing lies...
So they will not cry...
        Sadly confused... In my mind high...
Heavenly... eye...
        torn between the two.... say bye-bye...
If they could read my mind...
        I'm doing' it just for you... As I stare deep
In-to both their eyes...

                          AVANT TYPE SONG

CHORUS: (REPEAST TWICE)   (53)

        I got... a wife and mis-tress...
I-got... a wife and mistress...
        Our love is complicated...
We're in love and I can't change it...

VERSE I:

        They smile... cause they don't know...
And I won't hurt them... Good-love... nice and slow...
        Pure e-motion... Up and down...
and back and forth... Sex-ing cra-zy...
        I truly love them both... They're my ba-bays.

BRIDGE/PREHOOK:

REPEAT CHORUS UNTIL MUSIC FADES OUT.

MID TEMPO

A LITTLE BIRD

VERSE I:
   Be careful what you say...
Ain't in the mood to-day...
   Cause I just heard... that you been
cross town... play-ing childish games...
   It's driv-ing me in-sane... (boy)
That you could act so lame... (lord)
   word got out, that you were
with one of your old flames...
   you look me in my face...
Like how I know these things...
   Won't run my mouth, you can't figure it out.
but the feds is on the case...

CHORUS: (REPEAT TWICE)   **(54)**
   No-don't worry about now... worry about how...
How I got my source...
   Know I heard it from a... Got it from a...
From a little bird...
   No-don't worry about now... worry about how...
I knew where you were...
   Say I heard it from a-little bird and...
I won't tell a word...

VERSE II:

   Why you wanna know the name...
of the one who said your name?
   You got caught and a little bird said...
you pass it everyday...
   And what seems to be so strange,
Is that you always say...
   Exactly what... that birdie told me...
you would probably say....

REPEAT CHORUS UNTIL THE MUSIC FADES OUT.

MID TEMPO

GREEN LIGHT

CHORUS:
    She giving me the green light (green light)...
Green light, go...
    So we can get it all night, (all night)...
all night... whoa...
    She giving me the green light, (green light)...
green light, go...
    And I'ma do it just-right, (just right)...
just right for her...

VERSE I:
    Room full of liquor... pocket full of rubbers...
Pedals on the covers... just for my lover...
    Boy I really want her... number one stunna...
wait a whole summer... to put some-thing on her...

BRIDGE/PREHOOK: (55)

    Ba-by... I-been... wait-ing... (did you hear me say?)
Ba-by... I-been... wait-ing... (I been show-ing the...)
    Sin-say... kind-of... patience... (you know I have the)
Sin-say... kind-of... patience...

VERSE II:
    Finally gonna' get her... Gin-zu split-her...
Back stroke swimmer... Real deep digger
    Af-ter dinner... gen-tle mister...
Take time wit-er... and make love wit-her....

BRIDGE/PREHOOK

REPEAT CHORUS UNTIL MUSIC FADES OUT.

SLOW

SLOW UP

VERSE I:

      We been... on dates... acup-la' times...
I have... to say... first-I was shy...
      Boy you're... so fine... you charge... my-vibe...
And I... couldn't of... met a more per-fect guy...

BRIDGE/PREHOOK:

      To-night... I... want... to take-it slow....
One... night... we... will... make-love... for sure...
      To-night... I... want... to take-it slow...
One... night... we ... will... make-love... for sure... so...

MELANIE FIONA TYPE SONG

CHORUS: (REPEAT TWICE)

      Slow it up... slow it up... slow it up... slow it up...
Boy slow up your pace... it's only our first date...
      Slow it up... slow it up... slow it up... slow it up...
Boy it's not a race... better if we wait...

VERSE II: **(56)**

      I like... the way... you wine-and dine...
Make no... mis-takes... it-feels just right...
      But time... will make... it-oh... so nice...
If you... can wait... I'll make you mine...

BRIDGE/PREHOOK:

REPEAT CHORUS UNTIL MUSIC FADES OUT.

MID

BLUSH

VERSE I:

        Boy-you... make-my smile-bright...
Tell-me where... did you come from..?
        Think-about you... all night...
All-day-long... and then-some...
        Ooh-it feels so right...
My heart-pound... bass drum.. (he make me)

CHORUS:

        Blush... so-hard... so-hard...
My God-he makes me...
        Blush... so-hard... so-hard...
Can't fight-the feel-ing...
        Blush... so-hard... so-hard...
See him here-is dearing...
        Blush... so-hard... so-hard...
Our love's ne-ver end-ing...

VERSE II: (57)

        Ooh-you make me-feel so...
spe-cial and so-fine...
        Raise-in my e-go... like
sunshine and sunrise...
        Give me the ex-treme flow...
goose-bumps thrill me-oh-my...
        In-hale smoke-and then blow...
Ex-hale babe-you so-fine...

BRIDGE/PREHOOK:

        It's just the way you-are...
that has me o-pen...
        It's just the way you touch me...
that keep's me blushing...

REPEAT CHORUS UNTIL MUSIC FADES OUT.

SLOW

IF I COULD

VERSE I:

        This life-should be... (life should be)(2)...
Like a-good mo-vie... (good mo-vie)(2)
        Live with no-worries... (no worries) (2)
Perfect Fan-ta-sy... (fan-ta-sy)(2)

BRIDGE/PREHOOK:

        It should be for-ever Va-len-tines...
Never have a day of a-ny crime...
        Together we would join our hands and rise...
And birth would be the only time we cry... (we cry)(3)

CHORUS:

        If I could change the world-I...
Would shape it like it should-be...
        make the people friend-ly...
Have it-so no one ev-er starve a-gain...
        If I could change the world I...
Would make it like it should-be...
        Spread the world with world-peace...
And we will never have a war again...

(58)

VERSE II: ADELE TYPE SONG

        The price of life-is cheap...
(life is cheap)(2)...
        For all-kill-ings... (all-kill-ings)(2)...
It is so silly... (so silly)(2)...
        Hard En-vy (hard en-vy)(2)...

BRIDGE:

REPEAT CHORUS UNTIL MUSIC FADES OUT.

POP

LOVE ENOUGH

INTRO:
        Love (love), love (love), lala (lala)…
Lala love…
        Love enough (love enough), love, love…
Love enough…

VERSE I:
        I don't know… I don't know…
If you really love me…
        If you don't… let me know…
And just-let me be…
        I am way… way to fly…
just to be… waste-ing…
        All the time… in the world…
And it's not for free…

NICKI MINAJ TYPE SONG

CHORUS: (59)

        You don't love… (you don't love)… you don't love e-nough…
        You don't love… (you don't love)… you don't love… e-nough…
        You don't love-love-love… you don't love e-nough…
        You don't love-love-love…you don't love e-nough

VERSE II:
        All my girls… show ya' hands…
if you-feel-ing me…
        Shout out to La-dy B…
putting on-a-ring…
        Where the dudes… with the girls…
Show-ing love cra-zy?
        And it's true… true romance…
feel-ing a-ma-zing…

REPEAT CHORUS UNTIL MUSIC FADES OUT.

POP

MISERY LOVES IT

CHORUS:

      S.O.L.O.N.E.L.Y. (MISERY).
S.O.L.O.N.E.L.Y (LOVES-LOVES).
      S.O.L.O.N.E.L.Y (COMPANY)
Misery lo-ves company, (company)...

VERSE I:

      You gotta lot of ish always going on...
You need to grow up... let go-and move on...
      Your vibe is bad... and everybody knows...
Nega-tiv-i-ty like poof be gone...

BRIDGE/PREHOOK:

      A lot of en-vy eating away slow-ly...
And that's the rea-son... you are so lonely...
      A lot of en-vy... wating away slow-ly...
Misery love... company (company)...

REPEAT CHORUS TWICE.

                                                                    (60)

VERSE II:

      You probably mad-and upset that you broke...
I know-you wish the whole world gag and choke...
      Your attitude is messed up...no smiles no jokes...
Get your heart right-wash your mouth with soap...

REPEAT CHORUS UNTIL MUSIC FADES OUT.

POP

EXPENSIVE

CHORUS:

       I-am expensive… check out-my purses…
Make-up-and-outfits… ring it up-charge it…
       I-am expensive… bat-ting my eye-lids…
Buy-the whole-outlet… if you-wan-na fat-kiss…

VERSE I:

       Pass-me-a-Chanel-hand-bag this way…
Christ-ian Lou-bou-tin-pumps buy me babe…
       Pra-da, fen-di, bur-ber-ry's o-k…
To-get-with-me-you have to know the game…

BRIDGE/PREHOOK:

       Sor-ry… but-it's… got-ta be… cent-ered around-lil ol me…
       The best… of things-in life-are free… but…that don't apply to me.

REPEAT CHORUS TWICE

(61)

VERSE II:

       Buy-me-a-new-ba-len-ci-a-ga… Gucci-and a shin-ey Car-tier…
       Bri…oni coat-ca-rri-bean-get away… Ruth Chris steak-and-Audemars-Pi-quet.

BRIDGE/PREHOOK:

REPEAT CHORUS UNTIL MUSIC FADES OUT.

POP/ALT/DANCE

CAT'S MEOW

CHORUS:
    Now-don't be jock-ing my cat's meow... meow (meow).
I see you stare-ing now break it down... it down (it down).
    Now don't be jockin' my cat's meow... meow (meow).
    We bout our business, we run this town... this town (this town).

VERSE I:
    Boy I'm con-troller bust a move... you see-dear...
    Name a spot-and bring your crew... I'll be there...
Mu-sic loud-the bass will boom... beat, beat clear...
    We so con-fident and cool... have no fear...

BRIDGE/PREHOOK:

    Oh... wee... oh... we drop it low...
We... go... deep-er than most...
    The show... you know we stole...
We stole... we stole... we stole...

REPEAT CHORUS TWICE   (62)

HEY VIOLET TYPE SONG

VERSE II:
    I'm bout ready lace up your shoes... we in here...
Trying to bite style from my crew... our tight gear...
    Super bouncie check our suits... the chicks stare...
D.J. turn it up... my crew lit ooh... be aware...

BRIDGE:

REPEAT CHORUS UNTIL MUSIC FADES OUT.

MID/UP TEMPO

CHEAPSKATE

INTRO/BRIDGE:
      Come on... come and spend something...
Come on... come and spend something...

VERSE I:
      You al-ways showing off... (showing off)...
But you and I really-know, (really know)
      Know what-you remind me of? (remind me of?)
A gangster in a studio, (studio)...
      I see... you rocking knock off's, (knock off's)...
Frontin' when you're really broke, (really broke)...
      I guess-you're what they're talking bout, (talking bout)...
      When they say... he ain't tippin' folks...
                 RHIANNA TYPE SONG

BRIDGE/PREHOOK
      Come on... come and-spend something...
Come on now... spend a little something...
      Come on... come and-spend something...
Come on now... spend a little something...

CHORUS: **(63)**

      Why you a cheapskate? I mean for Pete's sake...
Why you a cheapskate? Cheap, cheap, cheap, skate...
      Why you a cheapskate? Don't want a cheap date...
      Why-you a cheapskate boy (boy), boy (boy)?

VERSE II:
      Got bus-iness running off, (running off)...
They're point-ing saying there he go, (there he go)...
      We al-ways spot you with, (spot you with)...
A-small group of silly hoes, (silly hoes)...
      You half-way try to floss, (try to floss)...
Watching them videos, (videos)...
      I caught you with a lot of that, (lot of that)...
Fake mo-ney for music videos, (videos)...

SLOW

NATURAL BEAUTY

VERSE I:

       Ooh… ba-by… You're so pre-tty…
and I had to let you know… that your sexy nat-ural…
       You… showed me… A wo-men's beau-ty…
I would like to give you a toast… a toast to what you have on…
       And I love you… for you-being you…
And the way you touch me-when I get home you still love me…
       It is so-true… like the smell of perfume…
Mother nat-ures beauty in you…

CHORUS: (REPEAT TWICE)   (64)

       She sittin' at home… with her panties on…
And a t-shirt on… with no make-up on her face…
       She sittin' at home… with her panties on…
And a t-shirt on… with no make up on her face…

VERSE II:

       She's…wait-ing… on her ba-by…
And she so beau-ti-ful… even with name brand fashion on…
       Bas-ic… sex-y… good smash-in babe…
And you already know… shirt and undies on the floor…

BRIDGE:

REPEAT CHORUS UNTIL MUSIC FADES OUT.

MID TEMPO

SO MAGNIFICENT

VERSE I:
        I'm... on... a miss-ion...
Top... speed... I'm trip-pin...
        Shoot for the best-when it's
my time...
        I... had... a vis-ion...
mixed with pre-cision...
        Some-laughed... but doubt
never crossed-my mind...

BRIDGE/PREHOOK:
        We... have... won... and it's cra-zy
oh-ba-by...
        A shin-ing sun... heat-ing up...
And it's a flam-ing...
        We... have... won... like the na-vy
(65)
oh ba-by...
        We... ain't... done... oh-no...
And guess what we're stay-ing..?

CHORUS: (REPEAT TWICE)
        So-mag-nificent... you're strange to us...
We're mag-nificent... changed the game on up...
        So-mag-nificent... can't hang with us...
We're mag-nificent... You on the same ol' stuff...
        (So magnificent)

VERSE II:
        Big money spend-ing...
The whole plan winn-ing...
        So we-can shine...
All majors deal-ing...
        Hell-uva feel-ing...
Liv-in this good...
        should be a crime...

BRIDGE UNTIL MUSIC FADES OUT.

SLOW/COUNTRY

80 REASONS

VERSE I:

        Lay-ing here... I count the ways...
You fill-your love... In-side my heart... (babe)
        Ma-ny days... I-want and crave...
the touch-and warmth... from your em-brace...
        Turn the page... for time you made...
Me your-love slave... wet in-the rain... (babe)
        And up-the same... each time-each phase...
for what-I'm proud... and it won't change...

CHORUS: (REPEAT TWICE)

        Eigh-ty rea-sons... Eigh-ty rea-sons...
Eigh-ty rea-sons... I can think of-why-I love you...
        Eigh-ty rea-sons... Eigh-ty rea-sons...
Eigh-ty rea-sons... I can spend my life with you...

VERSE II: (66)

        When-you're away... I call-your name...
In retrospect-I stay on your brain...
        Games-we play... Our love-insane...
Our love will raise-and it won't change...
        I can't explain... so much to gain...
In time we lay... I smile for days...
        Ace of spades... One in eight-ty...
My heart is chained... you got me babe...

REPEAT CHORUS UNTIL MUSIC FADES OUT.

SLOW

I AIN'T FINNA

VERSE I:

    Lone-ly I… been all-this win-ter…
Be-cause you… been gone since no-vember…
    Tea-ry eyes… cry-in a ri-ver…
And-I had no one to wipe-them…

BRIDGE:

    I gave-my heart… and soul to you…
My mind… and my time… be-longs to you…
    So I… de-cide to dis-miss you…
Be-cause you hurt me babe…

CHORUS: (REPEAT TWICE)

    I ain't finna' keep… Tak-ing you back…
Ba-by I… sure-ly did miss you…
    Late at night… I hear whis-pers…
Your voice-call in me nearer…

VERSE II: (67)

    Late-ly I… would stare at your pic-ture…
Ba-by I… sure-ly did miss you…
    Late at night… I hear a whis-per…
Your voice-call in me near-er…

BRIDGE:

    I want-ed all… the world for you…
And eve-ry breath that I take… for you…
    All of these signs appeared true…
So how could you… keep on leav-ing me…

REPEAT CHORUS UNTIL MUSIC FADES OUT.

SLOW/MID

THIS JOURNEY

CHORUS:

           On this road... (on this road)...
Of this jour-ney... (jour-ney)...
           Where it goes for sure...
No one real-ly knows...
           On this road... (on this journey)...
Of this jour-ney... (jour-ney)...
           E-ven through the storm...
We keep mov-ing on...

VERSE I:

           The road is long... and the streets are packed...
the trail is gone... ain't no way back...
           You're go-ing in... It's the drive-within....
No choice-but to win... there's no rematch...
           It's not the come-up... It's the bounce back...
Never give up... keep it on track...
           They treat you so wrong... you fought for so long...
When you get there... you earned that...

CHORUS: (REPEAT TWICE)   (68)

VERSE II:

           The path we're on... is the hard-est...
Stay in a zone... the strong will out-last...
           You squeeze a stone... crush it like glass...
In the open-ed hand... brings dia-monds back...
           You al-most home... al-most fin-ished...
The lights are strong... shine you'll win...
           Grind to the bone... and don't look back...
We're on cruise con-trol... they can't take it back...

REPEAT CHORUS UNTIL MUSIC FADES OUT.

SLOW

SLEEPING WITH HER

VERSE I:
        We... start-ed out as friends...
Date... ing-now and then...
        She... was the one-I could de-pend...
on... over, (and over) a-gain...
        De-velop-ing... e-mo-tions...
I-guess... time will al-ways win...
        Once... we looked-in to each-others...
eyes... next-thing you know-we start to kiss...

CHORUS:
        Everything was cool... until I started
Sleep-ing-with-her, (sleep-ing with-her)...
        Might of changed the rules...
When I started sleep-ing with-her (sleep-ing with-her)...
        I made a bad move... when I started...
Sleep-ing with-her (sleep-ing with-her)...

VERSE II: (69)
        E-mo-tions start to clash-cause...
she knows-all the other girls that I had...
        And... the story doesn't end...
cause now-she wanna no where I been...
        I miss the time we had before sex-in...
I learned a very valuable less-on...
        Don't under-estimate the bless-ings...
of a spe-cial friend no question...

BRIDGE: (REPEAT TWICE)
        The trust we had, (the trust we had).
Came to an end, (came to an end).
        Very bad, (very bad).
To lose a friend, (to lose a friend).

REPEAT CHORUS UNTIL MUSIC FADES OUT.

MID TEMPO

FOOT FETTISH

VERSE I:

       Baby gotta strut... Shaw-tay tough...
Ba-by yeah-in them jeans... calves and butt...
       So I roll up... just my luck...
She see me... eye-ing her... dan-ger-ous...
       La-dy what's up... ain't seen you a-round...
What's your name? Where you from? Cat's meow...
       Digg-ing your smile... Scale-in-down...
Hair weave check... gear on deck... shoe game-wow...

CHORUS:

       She-got some pre-tty toes... (pre-tty toes)...
Got me buy-ing sti-le-ttoes... (sti-le-ttoes)...
       Treat her to a ped-i-cure... (ped-i-cure)...
And she gave me a fashion show...
       She got some-pre-tty toes... (pre-tty toes)...
And I got a fet-tish for...
       Like the way them plat-forms stroll (2)...
Man I got-a fett-ish bro...

VERSE II: (70)

       Take-ing her to shop... till we drop...
Louie this... Prada that... ba-by hot...
       Shoes on stock... we're going to cop.
Chosing the one, to wear, no socks.
       I got me a crush... Roy-al flush...
Hold-ing hands... just the two... two of us...
       She likes a foot rub... I show love...
So I touch... foot fett-ish, (foot fett-ish)...

REPEAT CHORUS UNTIL MUSIC FADES OUT.

                                                                    SLOW

IN YOUR WORLD

VERSE I:

        Are you… a su-per mo-del..?
A fam-ous… mo-vie star..?
        I'll bet… a hun-dred bot-tles…
you are… you are… you are…
        How bout I let you bor-row…
The key that un-locks my heart..?
        A life-of love… will fol-low…
And I… won't ev-en change…

CHORUS:

        How can I… get in your world..?
Your so fine… Let me know girl…
        How can I… get to know you girl..?
And spend some time… in your world?
        How can I… get in your world?
You're a dime… I'm a flirt girl…
        How can I… get to know you girl…
and give you… all-the world..?

VERSE II: (71)

        It's like… I hit the lot-to…
You are… the best-thus far…
        You kill… like semi-auto…
And you-shine like fancy cars…
        Your beauty makes me follow…
I hear an angel's harp…
        To spoil you… is the mot-to…
When would-you like to start…

REPEAT CHORUS UNTIL MUSIC FADES OUT.

MID

YOUR GIRL

CHORUS:

        I've been wanting to ask... to be your-girl...
Want it more than bad... than all the world...
        Our loves go-nna last... a pre-cious pearl...
I been wan-na ask... to be your girl...

VERSE I:

        I... saw-our love... in a dream...
All cuddled up... just you and me...
        Per-fect match... what you think? Hurt so good... bit-ter sweet...
        In-my mind... you're a king... how can I... be your queen..?
        Lock-my heart... be with me... cause you-got... Got the key...

CHORUS: (REPEAT TWICE) (72)

VERSE II:

        I... saw our love... our love-in dream... there we were... fan-ta-sy...
        Over seas... on a beach... only us... In a bed... between the sheets... mak-ing love...
        Sent from a-bove... like a note that's brought... And de-livered... from a dove...
        My heart beats... it's filled with love... and I just wanna give... if you want love... so...

REPEAT CHORUS UNTIL MUSIC FADES OUT.

SLOW

DREAM ABOUT YOU

VERSE I:

        Lay-in here... in my bed-all alone...
Wrapped inside my sheets....
        I just woke up... I'm in my zone...
Stare-ing at-the ceiling fan...
        Mov-ing slow... It's half past four...
And I... can't sleep no, (I can't sleep no-more)...

BRIDGE/PREHOOK:

        You give me butter-flies in-side...
I felt it in my dream... through the sky...
        The magical cloud is nine...
We're the King and Queen...

        TONI BRAXTON TYPE SONG

CHORUS: REPEAT TWICE　　　　　　　　(73)

        The o-ther day... I had a dream about you, (dream about you).
And-now-I... been hav-ing feel-ings bout you, (feel-ings bout you).
        The o-ther day... I had a dream about you, (dream about you).
Cra-zy how... I can't stop think-ing bout you (think-ing bout you).

VERSE II:

        The love we share... I in-vest in so strong...
Open up my... mind and heart then... I'm dream-ing on...
        Fantasize-mesmerized-got me gone... wake-ing up I'm all smiles-cause you love me so...

BRIDGE:

REPEAT CHORUS UNTIL MUSIC FADES OUT.

POP

BORN AND BRED

VERSE I:
        See... the bright lights flash-ing...
See-the fancy clothes-and cars...
        Da-zzle-ing out lasting...
Any challengers thus far...
        Super-duper family...
Won't be none... don't you start...
        In the club-excit-ing...
Plus, we bought the bar...

BRIDGE/PREHOOK:

        And we do it... yeah we do it-do it...
We're the tru-est... we're the tru-est to it...
        And we do it... yeah we do it-do it...
We're the tru-est ...re-main tru-est to it...

REPEAT CHORUS TWICE (74)

        Born-in-Amer-ica... Bred in Amer-ican...
Grub at my favorite spots... Ball at the mall and spend...
        Born-in Amer-ica... Bred ub Amer-ican...
Home-of the che-vy truck... land-of the Ben-jamin's...

VERSE II:
        Yeah... our life out-standing...
mo-vie stars... ex-pen-sive cars...
        Po-verty and class-y... pro-ject life-
mansions big yards...
        Char-donnay and Bran-dy... in the club
buy out the bar...
        And we fine-so dandy... kind-a like a Hall
Mark card...

BRIDGE/PREHOOK:

REPEAT CHORUS UNTIL MUSIC FADES OUT.

SLOW

<u>*HIS LADY*</u>

CHORUS:

      I'm his la-dy... He's my ba-by...
I'm not changing... And I want you to know...
      I'm his la-dy... And he's my ba-by...
And you won't change me... so I need you to go.

VERSE I:

      Greet-ing card... broke-n heart...
Un-expect-ed visit, he wait-ing on my car...
      We won't start... griev-ing hard...
It's sure an issue... if he finds out who you are...
      I hope you are... o-ver our... last and
final-break-up... that left us scarred...
      This is odd... so please stop... text-ing me
with questions... cause I'm in love...

REPEAT CHORUS TWICE: **(75)**

VERSE II:

      Shoot-ing stars... way past mars... cupid
shot an arrow... landing in my heart...
      Some try hard... I-swear-I'm deeply dedicated
Don't care who you are... He's by far... past the stars...
      Of my past relations.... I had thus far...
Get-ting dark... I should start... Driving to my baby...
      Hope-you find your heart....

REPEAT CHORUS UNTIL MUSIC FADES OUT.

POP

SHAKE DOWN

VERSE I:
        We at the bar...
We look-ng sex-y...
        Me and my girls...
But his eyes-on me...
        He don't know me...
Have-ing the Bat-ten-der...
        send us drinks...

BRIDGE/PREHOOK :   (76)
        On the dance floor... I drop-it-roll-ing...
He check-ing my skills... I'm stare-ing bold-ly...
        He's to aggressive, so I act cold-ly...
Mus-ic is bang-ing loud...

CHORUS: (REPEAT TWICE)
        He wan-na shake me down... (he wan-na shake me down) He wan-na shake me down...
        (he wan-na shake me down)   He wan-na take me... try-ing to break me...
        He wan-na shake me down... (he wan-na shake me down)

VERSE II:
        Check my Bvl-gar-i...
we still in the par-ty...
        And is still packed...
wall to wall-with the hot-ties
        I like it when they...
Be call-ing me Shaw-ty...
        We in the A...
Sweat-ing, danc-ing, real naugh-ty...
        He's cross-ing the dance floor...
of the party... Tak-ing my hand... lead the way.....
        Dance-ing up on me... I feel...
when he's grind-ing...

REPEAT CHORUS UNTIL MUSIC FADES OUT.

POP
SO CAN I

VERSE I:

      This is-my theme song (theme song)...
Watch how-I do it (do it)...
      I'm going to blow up... spark up the fuses (fu-ses)
Just turn my beat up (beat up)... ain't noth-ing to it (to it)
      Been study-ing so long (so long). Vi-deo music (mu-sic)...

BRIDGE I:

      Ambitions so high (so high)...
Turn up like speakers (speak-ers)...
      I'm next in the chow-line (chow-line)...
Care-ful might eatcha (eatcha)...
      Right place and right time (right time)...
Ya'll better keep up (keep up)...
      Success and a nice life (nice life)...
Ben-z's and Beem-ers (beem-ers)...

CHORUS: (77)

      If you... can do it-so can I...
with-out wings... soar through the sky...
      like a holly-wood star shines...
If you can do-it, so-can I...
      Any-thing that cross the mind...
Turn a pen-ny to a dime...
      If you can do it than-so can I...

VERSE II:

      I get my grind on (grind on)...
Love com-petition (-tition)...
      No time for whine-in (whine-in)...
I'm on a mission (miss-ion)...
      Doubt me your dead wrong (dead wrong)...
Persistence viscious (viscious)....
      Fell ma-ny times now back again...
bred with commit-ment...

SLOW

TEN TIMES

VERSE I:

   Let me tell you bout (love)...
Let me tell you bout (sweet love)...
   Sex-ing my queen...(up)...
Her beau-ties a beast (huh..?)
   She be call-ing me freak-em...
Man you should of (seen us)...
   The way that we were... breathe-ing...
And sweat-ing them sheets...(up)...

CHORUS: (78)
   last-night... she came o-ver...
Last-night... feel-ing on her...
   Last-night... we got closer...
We made love... ten times over...
   Last-night... she came o-ver...
last-night... we got closer...
   Last-night... feel-ing on her...
We made love... ten times o-ver...

JAGGED EDGE TYPE SONG

VERSE II:
   It got a little (rough)...
Shawty couldn't get e-nough...
   Switch-ing them posi-tions up...
She's all that I be think-ing of...
   She a helluva sis...ta...
Sexy lips I like to kiss...'em...
   Only one miss-ion... to have...
her flow-ing like riv-ers....

ALT/POP

HAPPY DAYZ

INTRO:

       We gotta think of... the Hap-py Day'z...
The Hap-py Day'z-keep-a smile-ing face...

VERSE I:

       Liv-ing free... have-ing fun...
Shine-ing bright... like the sun...
       Trick or treats... we were young...
Show-ing love to every-one...
       No wor-ries... change will come...
Stand-ing proud... cause we won...
       Remember-ing... bubble yum...
Hide and seek... and water guns...

CHORUS:

       We gotta think of... the hap-py day'z...
The hap-py day'z... keep a smile-ing face...
       I still think–of the hap-py day'z...
The hap-py day'z...and the point it made.

VERSE II: (79)

       In our teens... grow-ing up...
Get into-all... types of stuff...
       Sometimes life... it was rough...
Overcame... by spread-ing love...
       Joy will bring... tons of love...
All be-cause we stood up...
       Just have faith... re-main tough...
Just remem-ber... how good it was...

REPEAT CHORUS UNTIL MUSIC FADES OUT.

POP

HOLOGRAM

INTRO:

    Ha-ah-lo-gram, (ha-ah-lo-gram)...
Ha-ah-ha-lo-gram, (ha-ah-ha-lo-gram)...

VERSE I:

    She-got her make-up on.
She's dance-ing to her favorite song.
    She's per-fect with-no... things wrong.
She got them double d's... hey...
    She-tease-these-boys-can't you see?
She's a decoy... res-cue me
    Lipo, implants, sur-gery.
Biggest its... I... ev-er seen...

BRIDGE: KESHA TYPE SONG

    Mu-sic takes me... that's my jam...
She's so fake-and filled with scams...'
    Mu-sic takes me... that's my jam...
She's so fake-and filled with scams.

CHORUS: (REPEAT TWICE)   (80)

    Sili-cone queen... she gets down...
She so sex-y... Ho-lo-gram...
    Nice shape-bust-ie... plastic round...
Fake eve-rything ... Ho-lo-gram...

BRIDGE:

VERSE II:

    Princes Duck lips isn't she...
She ain't what she use to be...
    Fine and pre-tty look at me...
All this nat-ural-bea...u...ty...

REPEAT CHORUS UNTIL MUSIC FADES OUT.

POP/DANCE

HITTIN' LIKE

INTRO:
        What it's hittin' like... show me what it's hittin' like...
        Wanna know it, boy you know it.... show me what it's hittin' like...

VERSE I:
        The bass is beat-ing... Wake who-ever sleep-ing... Dance to the mu-sic... Par-ty for the week-end...
        Jam any season... Don't need any reason... It's a ce-lebra-tion, no...bo-dies leave-ing...

BRIDGE/PRE-HOOK

        Show how you do...it-don't be shy... Show how you do... it-don't be shy....
        Mu-sic blast-ing, hands up high... So lit, good-time, hands up high...

CHORUS: (REPEAT TWICE)   (81)

        What it's hittin' like... show me what it's hittin' like.
        Wanna know it, boy you know it, show me what it's hittin' like.
        I know the mood right... and I see you groove nice...
        Show you know it, boy you know it, show me what it's hittin' like...

VERSE II:
        Plenty drink-ing... three days going in... Hey they're rave-ing cra-zy... let's begin...
        Way past ten the crowd just coming in... Party (party), party, till the end...

REPEAT CHORUS UNTIL MUSC FADES OUT.

POP

NO MORE

CHORUS:

        I'm-not...with your-cheat-ing no more...
I don't... want to hear no reasons no more....
        I'm-not with your-cheat-ing no more...
I don't care to hear it no more...

BRIDGE I:

        I'm finally gonna leave you...
It's been so much we been through...
        I don't wann hear your story...
Now be gone-cause you di-squst me...

VERSE I:

        I... re-call... you say... you loved me...
What... I saw... was ve-ry ugly...
        I... don't wan-na hear... your story...
Now be gone... dude-you disqusting...

BRIDGE II:

        My hearts-in lit-tle pieces...
My hearts-in lit-tle pieces...

VERSE II: (82)

        This... will be... your last... story...
All... the ly-ing... start-ing to bore me...
        Sip...ping on... some kind... of whiskey...
Then... I go... find some... one to love me...
        I feel...a-li-ttle some-thing...
A heart-breaks hard to take...
        I'll find a par-ty jumping...
And I'm gonna cel-e-brate...

REPEAT CHORUS UNTIL MUSIC FADES OUT.

POP

THE SURPRIZE

CHORUS:

    I... love a sur-prise (sur-prise)...
Ex-cite... right...
    Give... me a surprise... bright lights...
Good times-fine...
    Make... it a sur-prise... tonight...
we ride high...
    I want my sur-prise (surprise)... out of site...

VERSE I:

    It's... my night... we're gonna toast...
Par-tay... dance until we explode...
    Feel... so right... grab... your coat...
Ha-ppy... yup-like we supposed.

BRIDGE:

    Sit... back... en-joy... no worries...
All...my friends... and fam-ily...
    Ce-le-brat-ing... yeah... we... ball-ing
close... my eyes... and–cheer-with-me...

CHORUS: REPEAT TWICE   (83)

VERSE II:

    Al-most time... here... we-go...
Rea-dy... pre-paring for the show...
  Guys... so lit... and madd peo-ple...
Par-tay all night live until they close...

BRIDGE:

CHORUS:

POP

WE GON' SHINE

BRIDGE/INTRO
        Shine (shine), shine (shine)...
On our grind, On our grind...
        Shine (shine), shine (shine)...
Par-ty time, (par-ty time)... Party...
VERSE I:
        Let's here-one for the-team...
We are liv-ing our dreams...
        No matter-how hard it seems...
Vic-tory... we worthy...
        Some helluva-kind of breed...
Must be mixed with ma-chines...
        We de-serve to be seen...
We have damn near con-quered everything...

BRIDGE: (REPEAT TWICE)   (84)
CHORUS:
        Damn-right we gon' shine... Like a star-high in the sky...
Damn-right we gon' shine... Till our spirits are shine-ing high...
        Damn-right we gon' shine... Be-cause it's our time...
That's right-we gon' shine... Be-cause it's our time...

        That's right- we gon' shine (gon' shine)...
Gon' shine, (gon' shine-like diamonds bright...)

VERSE II:
        They tried-calling us weak...
Til we conquered de-feat...
        We fight-hard and we bleed...
My eyes blurred I can't see...
        And now where in the lead...
Reign supreme King's and Queens...
        Now we want you to see...
How we shine with the team...

POP/ALT

FEAR NO THING

VERSE I:

        I... will have-no fear... of the dark-ness...
Dwell... the burn-ing sands... with no compass...
        lead the wound-ed troops... across the land...
Blood-on my hands-gripping the Ameri-can flag...
        I... will have-the heart... of a li-on...
Ba...ttle to the death... with a giant...
        Ig...nore all ther hurt... won't shed a tear.
Fight-ing for my life-until the end I near...

CHORUS: (REPEAT TWICE)

        I won't fear-no... thing... at all...
Give all I-got... Stand-ing tall...
        I won't fear-no... thing... at all...
Fight to the end... and will... not....
        fall (fall), fall at all...

(85)
VERSE II: MAROON 5 TYPE SONG

        I... will hold the fort... till the morning...
Swim the high-est tides-while it's storm-ing...
        Mo-ti-vate the team... in case tomorrow brings...
The evil nightmares from our dreams...
        Hold... in on my pride... till the world ends...
Land... of the brave... the ea-gles spoke-n...
        See... the red, the white, the blue, focus...
Let-ting all the world know-the U.S. is un-broken...

REPEAT CHORUS UNTIL MUSIC FADES OUT.

SLOW

FIRST SITE

VERSE I:

      I'm-lost in ya'-gaze... come and save-may...
My-heart was stole away... then-traded...
      Fate-brought... us to-this place... lovely la-day...
How long... will it-take... to be my... ba-bay..?

BRIDGE:

      Excuse me, but to me your so fine... you blew my mind...
      You're so-unique like sunshine... I won't lie...
Stand-ing next-to me is all I... see in our life...
      Honest... doe-like eyes... are just right...

CHORUS: (REPEAT TWICE)

      Love... at... first... site... (1)
Zoomed in... seen it... (1)
      Love... at ...first... site... (1)
You... won't believe it... (1)

VERSE II: **(86)**

      My-eyes... are scope-ing you... In amaze-ment...
True love... over-due... sex-y laday...
      I'm-so... In-to you... it is-cra-zay... one-heart...
for two-in love-help me make it....

BRIDGE:

REPEAT CHORUS UNTIL MUSIC FADES OUT.

SLOW

UP AT NIGHT

VERSE I:

      Toss and turn-ing... trust been brok-en... los-ing focus... bridges burn-ing...

BRIDGE:

      I'm in love... I'm in love... She took my trust... And I'm torn up...
      I'm in love... I'm in love... She took my trust... And shook me up...

CHORUS: (REPEAT TWICE)   **(87)**

      I can't eat... I can't sleep... up all night... Think-ing bout my dream...
      I can't eat... I can't sleep... think-ing bout Whatchu done to me...

VERSE II:

      Words not spoken... ain't no cope-ing... nose wide o-pen... I'll keep roll-ing.
      Heart keep hurt-ing... stress not work-ing... I've been
smoke-ing head ex-plode-ing.

BRIDGE:

VERSE III:

      I won't com-mit... never a-gain... Should of knew... when... she left her man...
      Why she do-it... I'm so fool-ish... Love so stupid... And I'm to pissed...
      Love's been lost... Love's been lost... We broke up, and it's all her fault...

REPEAT CHORUS UNTIL MUSIC FADES OUT.

MID/ALT

WE RALLY ON

VERSE I:

      Here's Cin-dy... Life to her is hopeless...
News on the tube... War got her focus...
      She's teary eyed... and heart broke-n...
She's not for sure...what's going wrong...
      Two months go by... with her pa-rents...
Mom starts to cry... Pop's baby grown...
      Her minds made up... The talk was worthless...
She mumbles out. Trust me I got this...

CHORUS: (REPEAT TWICE)

      You gotta be bold... you gotta be strong...
Hard as stone... And then we can rally on...
      Claim-ing the throne... mak-ing it known...
We won't fold... And then we rally on...

(88)

VERSE II:
      Regis-tered now... into the service...
Her palms begin to sweat... she's kinda nervous...
      Hope that no one notice... Her heart beat
searches... around for courage...
      Arm-y pla-toon... suits and boots... prepared for war...
      little soldier... to you sa-lute...

BRIDGE/PRE-HOOK:

      Don't wo-rry... God will hold me... just wish-the best for me...
      Don't worry... I'll be back shortly... yearning... to help my country...

REPEAT CHORUS UNTIL MUSIC FADES OUT.

SLOW/MID

<u>IT'S BEST I LEAVE</u>

CHORUS:
    I gotta go... I'm outta here...
I gotta go... Disappear...
    I gotta go... far from here...
Because she loves more than me...
    I gotta go... disappear...
I need to go... I think-cause
    I think it's best I leave...

VERSE I:
    It started bout a week ago...
Seen her friend at the corner store...
    I wish I never seen her though...
Cause she was tell-ing me ev-ery (tell-ing me every-thing)...
    Just came home... alone... baby girl
left her phone...I'm curious and want to know...
    So I open up (open up), open up
the touch screen.

BRIDGE: **(89)**
    Helluva way to find out... see my girl laying
on the couch...
    Not only was she stepping out... but
she video taped it (video taped it).

CHORUS: (REPEAT TWICE)

VERSE II:
    Soon as she came in tho... I showed her clip of
the private show...
    She acted like she seen a ghost... Then she
flipped
out on me (flip the thing back on me)...
    We're scream–ing at a high tone...I'm so mad I
could
chew brick stone...
    It's over gotta let-her now... That I gotta leave,
leave leave, (gotta leave her alone).

SLOW

I DON'T WANT HIM

CHORUS:

      In my-head... in my-head... I been through with that... You can have him back...
      In my-head... in my-head... I been through with that...I don't want him back...

VERSE I:

      Hold up... tie up-ya' tongue... one sec'... before you keep on...
      Last night... you called-my phone... first place... Where you went wrong...
      I got... bet-ter things... to do... then play... games... and fool around with you...
      Know that... you-seemed confused... Because a man... do-what he wanna do...

BRIDGE:

      You bet-ter.... get you some get right... You should... be get-ting your man right...
      You bet-ter... get you some get right... Heart breaks... can mess up... your whole life.

CHORUS: (REPEAT TWICE)   (90)

VERSE II:

      I'm done... Life goes on... I'm set... And I'ma keep on...
      No bum... could ev-er come... break my pride... No one...
      Let'em run... have some fun... a new day... A new love...
      Ask your mom... to teach you love... before you... get hurt..

REPEAT CHORUS UNTIL MUSIC FADES OUT.

SLOW

WATCH

CHORUS:

        Sweet-heart... watch you love me (watch you love me).
Ba-by watch you love me (watch you love me).
        Be my one and only (one and only).
Be my one and only (one and only)
        Ba-by watch you love me (watch you love me)
La-dy watch you love me (watch you love me)
        Never leave you lone-ly (never lone-ly)
Never leave you lone-ly (never lone-ly)

VERSE I:

        Here we go... here we go... right by my side....
Feel-ing you...eyes
        Ba-by brown eyes... smile so cute... girl you so fine... Sexy too...
        Yeah-I'm bold... (yeah-I'm bold) you caught my eyes... You been chose...
        To the sky high... we can go... I'll treat-you right... Give you my soul...

CHORUS: (91)

VERSE II:

        Let it flow... let it flow... feel my soul... Caress-ing you...
        Won't waste ya' time... I'm not a fool... won't you be mine... I'll say I do...
        Buy you clothes... An-y store... beau-ti-ful... So we can go...
        Dance-ing all night... And-buy a rose... to cater to you... one day propose.

REPEAT CHORUS UNTIL MUSIC FADES OUT.

SLOW/MID

NO MORE KISSES

VERSE I:
When you go-out-of that-door... I'm not sure... If you come-ing back...
Say you going to the store... it'll be two days... before you make it back...
I know it's my fault-that I played... and laid... and stayed... now I'm feel-ing that...
The emotion that I crave... been replaced... Plenty slack...

BRIDGE/PRE-HOOK:
It's your attitude-that express your mood... Early warning clues...
It's your attitude-that'll make you do silly things you do...
It's your attitude-got you acting rude... Playing me's not cool...
Leads-me to add the fact-with conclusions that keep me ask-ing why..?

CHORUS: REPEAT TWICE
We don't even kiss N.E. more... I feel like it's o-ver, o-ver...
How come we don't kiss N.E. more... He must want it to be o-ver (o-ver)....
We don't even kiss N.E. more... I feel like it's o-ver, o-ver...
He don't try and kiss me no more... I'm feel-ing like it's o-ver (o-ver)...

VERSE II:
I have given you-my house... keys... after my mom-said,"don't you shack."
What you say is make-believe... promise things... It's a lot of crap... Use to bright-en up my day... Now you cold... That's how you act...

MID TEMPO
BIG MONEY

VERSE I:
        I can tell by your shoes baby...
Super clean and match with it...
        I ain't trying to be rude hear may...
Diamond rollie telling what time it is...
        Your confident and cool with it...
One love... I feel a little cocki-ness...
        I know all about the counterfeit...
And that ain't this babe you smell legit...

BRIDGE/PRE-HOOK   SAGE-T TYPE SONG
        Unfold your bankroll now (now)(6)...
Boy-come with it...
        I wanna see the dough now (now)(6)...
Go-come with it...
        I hear you hot around town(6)... Boy-come with it...
        You got money by the pound(6)... Just-limmie see it...

CHORUS: (93)
        I hear you got big money (money) (1)...
Go boy and show me that money(money) (1)...
        I know you got big money(money)...
Show me-that money(money) (1)...
        What you gonna do for me(for me)...
Li-mmie see the money(money) (1)?

VERSE II:
        Every-thing brand new baby...
Popping hella litty know what time it is...
        The new shoes on the coup hear me...
Cus-tom made shine-ing rims per-fect... fit...
        You're not rich then your close to it...
Cop champagne large-ly... crates and cases...

BRIDGE:

REPEAT CHORUS UNTIL MUSIC FADES OUT.

UP TEMPO/DANCE

MOVE AND DIP

CHORUS:
      When I move you move, when I dip you dip.
When I roll like this, then you grab my hips.
      When I step this way, and you step don't trip.
I can dance all night feel-ing good don't quit.

VERSE I:

      Catch me the music flow...
The rhythm keep me in control...
      I like to work it, drop it slow...
Like dancers sliding down the poll...
      Can you catch me..? Feeling kind of sexy-
Catch up-with me if you can-come grab my hand and...

CIARA TYPE SONG

CHORUS (REPEAT TWICE)

VERSE II: (94)

      I like the way you're digging me...
where gigging in a zone...
      Your Ver-sace cologne...
with the beat it turns me on.
      I had some cocktails...
Arm-adale, grooving to the song.
      Till the break of down-outlasting spinning round
while lights is flashing in.

REPEAT CHORUS UNTIL MUSIC FADES OUT.

UP TEMPO/DANCE

I CAN TELL

INTRO:
        I can tell that-you light weight like me.
I can tell how-your eyeballs follow me.
        I can tell how-you want my bo-dy.
I can tell-right away that I turn you on.

VERSE I:
        Ooh! I think-I caught- a winner.
Five foot ten inch-big... tipper.
        Like the prince found-the gla...ss slipper.
I can sale you-my charm-quicker...
        Got the soul of-a blu....es singer...
With the moves of, a strip teaser.
        Known to make-the pumping strong heart weaker.
And the chase in your drink-sweeter.

CHORUS: (95)
        I can tell that-you light weight like me.
I can tell how-your eyeballs follow me.
        I can tell how-you want my bo-dy.
I can tell right-away that I turn you on.
        I can tell that-you think I'm sexy.
I can tell that-you'll kiss ne soft-ly.
        I can tell right-away that I turn you on.

VERSE II:

        Hey you! cat got-your tongue? Speak up.
You look well kept-fl..y chiefer.
        Sipping wine-caught your eye-seeker.
Gucci frames-on-this fine-sister.
        Slip and slide-then the grind-cheat-em.
Now I feed on your mind-eat up.
        Sexy thighs on my side-Libra.
Catch the prize-on this dime... diva.

REPEAT CHORUS UNTIL MUSIC FADES OUT.

MID TEMPO

OUT MY WINDOW

CHORUS:
                My music's on low... I hear the bass blow...
Zoned out-stare-ing... out my window...
                I miss my peo-ple-on my pillow...
Spaced out-glance-ing out my window.

VERSE I:
                My baby so fine... All on my mind...
I'm his moon-and he's my sunshine...
                Playback-rewind... Ribbon in the sky...
He's been gone... this how I past time.
                Lone-ly so I... Bump that old Shai...
The very next time... he'll be my...
                friends can see why... I love my guy...
On my pillow and sheets-green lime...
                Dazed but see fine... love is so blind...
Re-me-ni-scent while I sip whine...
                Songs of all kind... Lyric-ally I'm...
Plus the mu-sic-helps me... get by.

CHORUS: (REPEAT TWICE)　　　　　　　　(96)

VERSE II:
                When I play my jams low...
And you hear the beat slow...
                Slow jam ring tones, free my-peo-ple...
We felt love poems-Lauren Hill on tour with
                Charlie Wilson. We had real fun-Keisha Cole
sung... On the soul train com-pe-ti-tion...
                Keri Hil-son-Mint Con-di-tion... 'Retha
Franklin... In ro-tat-tion...
                Adjust my bass and... get to think-ing...
12 for the right-o-ccassion...
                My heart race-ing systems play-ing for my
baby I'll be wait-ing.

REPEAT CHORUS UNTIL MUSIC FADES OUT.

SLOW

BRO-KEN HEARTZ

INTRO/CHORUS:
       Bro-ken Heartz... (Bro-ken heartz)...
Gon' give me my keys-my-cars to my jeep...
       How it's gon' be.... and-please... just let me be...

VERSE I:
       You asked my name-and my number...
Your convo strange-like cold summers.
       Deuce burn rubber...
(I threw the deuce burn rubber).
       Hate so lame... cause hate don't love her...
My heart feels pain... and you don't have one...
       Peace burn rubber- I threw the deuce-burn rubber.

BRIDGE/PRE-HOOK:
       We can get it poppin' to the break of day...
Everyone you see me with not one-is fake...
       Tell the d.j. gon' and throw it up-more bass...
You ain't tryna love me then get out-my way...
       You're only telling half of the story...
Don't give me no excuse-cause you bore me...
       My space ship-stay filled with gas...
No I'm so hurt... feeling sad...

CHORUS: (REPEAT TWICE)

VERSE II:
       Caught up in... soul-Ties. (Caught up in... soul ties)...No more cries... No lies. (No more cries... no lies)...
       Caught up in... soul-ties. (Caught up in... soul ties)...I won't let you play my mind-If you leave-I will be fine.
       I ain't in the mood today... I really can't deal today...
       Plant-ing all of these seeds-how-we was gon' be Jigga and Be'.
       Will you please... just let me be...?

SLOW

FORBIDDEN WORDZ

VERSE I:

      Ar-gue-ing snce... the break... of dawn... fuss all night... we car-ry on...
      Go-in through... the per-fect storm... can't be...lieve my heart-is gone...
      Can-it be... a wo-man's scorn,,, is-it just... A part-we grown...
      Went-to far... the da-mage done... she won't move...   And I won't budge...

CHORUS: (REPEAT TWICE)

      Girl-we said... what should'nt be said... Forbidden was said... and things-was said...
      No matter who said... or when who said... the wordz-was said... we said'em.

VERSE II: **(98)**

      Forced into... an emp-ty space... tell... me how... It got-this way...
      Word-loud... ever-ry day... should we-leave... how could we stay...
      Ang-ry looks... that's on your face... mixed with pain... and it- won't change...
      Throw-in all... these years-away... can't be fixed... and it's a shame...

REPEAT CHORUS UNTIL MUSIC FADES OUT.

MID

MAKE MY BODY

VERSE I:

        Hey-boy... break me off some-thing...
you got-what I'm want-ing... (all through the night)
        Take my... love and then rub-it... touch it
and rub-it... cause you do it right...
        Good-vibes... flow through my sto-mach...
Yours when you-want it... I'll keep it tight...
        Cat's-eyes... see what you-watch-ing...
Climb up the mountain... (you keep me high).

CHORUS: (REPEAT TWICE)

        Make my bo-dy purr... I know...
you want... my love...
        Make by bo-dy purr... I long...
a touch... that's warm...

VERSE II: **(99)**
        I'm yours... got me all open...
feel-ing your motion... just you and I...
        This time... we don't need cau-tion...
This one is flaw-less. For real a dime...
        Divine... silence is broken...
Hold-ing and moan-ing... Damn you so fine...
        Feel fine... heart throbbing moment...
come-ing to... own it... sex-ing my mind.

REPEAT CHORUS UNTIL MUSIC FADES OUT.

SLOW

LOVE SHOP

VERSE I:

    I got-a few... a-head... of you... babe...
    I got-some of... the best-love... for... you-girl...
    You'll have-the new... feel... real so-on yeah...
    Be-tween your thighs... smoove beg-ging for more...

BRIDGE/PRE-HOOK

    I aim... to have-you o-pen... for all... those-heart broken...
    No cost-to you... Put it down that's what I do.

CHORUS: (REPEAT TWICE)   **(100)**

    At the-love... shop... al-way's o-pen... Love... shop... ne-ver- close-ing...
    Love... shop... serve-ing you... Ba-by what-can I do for you?
    The love shop... Al-ways o-pen... Love shop-never close-ing...
    Love shop... how you do..? You're so fine-can I please help you..?

VERSE II:

    Go spread-the news... my crew work to babe...
    We grind all day... snow... hail... heat... and rain...-yeah...
    Kick off-your shoes... let me-freak you la-day...
    On-your mark... hit your spot... have it your way hey...

MID

TRIALZ TRIBULATIONS

CHORUS/INTRO:

      Going through changes... patience wasted... Life's outrageous-trials and tribulations...
      Wait-ing on wages. Hard times ain't it? Awkward stages-trials and tribulations...

VERSE I:

      Don't you know it? Seize the moment... Search-ing for...some-thing-very few people own.
      Friends is golden-sort of foreign-things don't seem...as there is-purpose for...
      Wallet stolen... Mortgage boken... keep on push-ing...like Rick Ross' song...
      Bills is roll-ing... family torn... we still are be-ing strongbarel hold-ing on...

CHORUS: (REPEAT TWICE)

VERSE II: (101)

      Heat is Blaze-ing... Police Taze-ing... people cra-zy... you must keep hold-ing on...
      Too much hate-ing... Fox's state-ments... Compli-cat-ing... this world, what's going on...
      Education... school's ain't change-ing... drop outs raise-ing... test scores keep fall-ing below...
      Kids is play-ing... Where they aim-ing... weapons crazy...'no love that's how it goes...

REPEAT CHORUS UNTIL MUSIC FADES OUT.

UP TEMPO/POP

BEHIND MY BACK

CHORUS:

      I heard you been talk-ing behind my back.
She say you say-I think I'm all of that.
      I al-ready knew-you were cut like that.
I won't act a fool. I won't flip on you.

VERSE I:

      I'm not really concerned what you have to say.
Cause I'm going to live my life any-way.
      Cause you don't feed my face and no bills you pay. So all the lies you tell all day's a waste.
      I don't really have time for a hater's hate.
Your below the earth-I'm out-ter space.
      I'm not the kind of girl-that makes or break.
You need to tone it down-no need to catch a case.

CHORUS: (REPEAT TWICE)   **(102)**

VERSE II:

      She say you say-you told me in my face.
But I don't even know you-by the way.
      The girl's with you are messy and they're fake.
It's the perfect click-yep filled with hate.
      I don't really have time for a hater's hate.
You are so beneath me-I... el-e-vate.
      I'm not the kind of girl words make or break.
You need to tone it down-before I catch a case.

REPEAT CHORUS UNTIL MUSIC FADES OUT.

POP

WATCH YOUR HOMEBOY

CHORUS:
  Better watch your homeboy-cause he tried to holler at me. Watch your (watch your) company-your boy tried to kick it to me.
  Better watch your homeboy-cause I caught him wink-ing at me.
Watch your (watch your) company-your boy tried to holler at me.

VERSE I:
  The only time-when you and I get to link up. Your with your boy-forever seems he's between us.
  Each time-he makes a move- he starts to sneak up. Turn your back a minute-he makes a move, right in front of you.
  I'm not the type to pass around. And if it's a game... I suggest we end it now.
  If it's not a game-the guy with you is fowl. And I think the boy is rude-why you keep the clown around?

CHORUS: (REPEAT TWICE)   (103)

VERSE II:
  One time-I just pretended not to see'em. He quick-ly-put more flirt in his demeanor.
  And leisurely-I tried to move and you seen us. And at the time, I was for sure you're working with him.
  Super Bowl, you had a little get together. You had to go-to the store you took forever.
  He winked his eye and tried to go a little further.
  Whispered low in my ear-"What he won't know won't hurt'em."

REPEAT CHORUS UNTIL MUSIC FADES OUT.

SLOW

YOUR BABIES MOTHER

CHORUS:
   You've been cheat-ing with your babies-mo-ther.
  I know because of this.
Your son said-you told her-you love her.
   and gave her a kiss.
You've been cheat-ing with your babies-mo-ther.
   And I remember when-She said that she would never-ever leave you again.

VERSE I:
   I should of known=from all the clues.
When you didn't do the things you use to do.
   Like I love you's-or some ballons.
A special night-the House Of blues.
   When you got the text-the text at two.
I ignored the signs-and kept my trust in you.
   I really love the kids. This is true.
What am I to do? I'm mad at you.

BRIDGE/PRE-HOOK: (104)
  What can I do? I'm sad so true...
What goes around comes back at you...
   It's just a shame. You're playing games...
You need to change cause...

CHORUS: (REPEAT TWICE):

VERSE II:
   Why are you playing-like I'm a fool?
With these silly game-like back in school.
   I overheard-you in the room...
sneak-ing around like your cool.
   When I try to talk-talk to you.
You brush me off-like I n=bother you.
   My love for you have been abused.
Really wanna cry-but who do I cry to?

UP TEMPO
SWITCH SPEEDS
CHORUS:
      I need you to switch speeds-catch up with me.
Cruising through this toll road-some pay fees.
      Start-ing off going slow mo-end full speed.
You can meet me at the finish line-don't beat me.
      I need you to switch speeds-catch up with me.
Ride-ing on the right-hot sparks-loud pipes.
      Even though the stretch tight-watch my lead.
You can meet me at the finish line-don't beat me.

VERSE I:
      I say he's like a bike-switching up like he's spose to. Because I need a man to keep up when it's time to.
      Not the kind of man-whining bout-how the flow moved.
You just grab the wheel-take control in the right mood.
      And be cool-pull out the right tool.
Work up a sweat-show me your best moves.
      I like to ride like I slide on a strip pole.
Ca-su-al sex-nope not a nympho.

BRIDGE: (105)
      It takes a lot of back when you move. Be cool.
You need a strong neck with it too. Be cool.
      You need long strokes with the groove. Be cool.
Before you get your-make sure I beat you. Beat you.

CHORUS: (REPEAT TWICE)
VERSE II:
      I can't even tell you the last time I came through.
The other dudes a lame-that's the rea-son I chose you.
      Hope you're not the same-six-feet with a small shoe.
I just copped a six-so you know-that I ball too.
      Let's race to-places that you like too.
Don't go to fast-always know-I have to beat you.
      The type of girl ride the clutch to the right tune.
Don't kill the mood-when I move come-ing to soon.

SLOW

SOMEONE ELSE

CHORUS:

    I'm in love with-someone-else too.
(I'm in love with someone else)
    I'm in love with-someone-else too.
(I'm in love with someone else)
    I'm in love with-someone-else too.
(I'm in love with someone else)
    I'm in love with-someone-else too.
(I'm in love with someone else)

VERSE I:

    It's been kind of quiet... we've been watching each other for weeks now.
    We had an office showdown... we made love on the company-couch.
    It felt so good-I know I should... go my own way.
    Plus I got my own baby- And I know- I love my a-day.
    I'm so confused-the way I'm fall-ing for you. Like you're my boo.
    I think about her and back to you... what am I gonna do?

                            FANTASIA TYPE SONG

CHORUS: (REPEAT TWICE)   **(106)**

VERSE II:

    This last past Monday. We finally started to talk-ing... and flirt-ing.
    Let me know for certain-it's not just about-humping around...
    Cause all though you got a man- and I got my girl.
I'm fall-ing deeper for you babe...
    And you make me feel a certain way.
What I need to know is-how am I going to keep being with you.
    And I feel good about the way... I'm loving you.

POP

DOCTOR (DOC-TOR)

CHORUS:

    Doctor (doctor) can you (can you)-get rid of this pain? Doctor can you get rid of it?
    I've been having pains flowing through my heart and my brain-since my baby went away.

VERSE I:

    Pass the Jim Beam cause the hurt is bumping through my dome. Sitting home all alone.
    Listen for the keys at the door-while I check my phone. I just cant believe that she's gone.
    Speakers on the radio blare-ing our favorite song. I still remember how she would moan.
    I have a fever can you feel my face? Damn doc what's wrong-can you prescribe-some patron?

BRIDGE I:

    I try to go to sleep-but I wake up with the same thing. All that I want is my baby (baby).
    I try to go to sleep-but I awake with the same thing. All I really want is my baby (baby).

CHORUS: (REPEAT TWICE)   **(107)**

VERSE II:

    I've had thoughts every since like Kurt Cobain. Her love was like a dose of cocaine.
    The way she had my heart-if I could I would tat' her name-inside of my chest save the pain.
    Can you give a dosage-stick a needle deep in my veins. Something to get rid of this thang?
    I see her pictures in your sleep-and in puddles when it rains. Baby got me going insane.

REPEAT CHORUS UNTIL MUSIC FADES OUT.

UP TEMPRO *(*

ON MY LAP

UP TEMPO

INTRO/PRE-HOOK:

     She bounce (bounce), bounce-the girl is all of that.
She bounce (bounce), bounce-the girl is on my lap.

VERSE I:

     Big boss ball-ing-pimp-ing in the club.
Off in here deep. The D.J. is showing love.
     Got bottles popp-ing-cham-pagne pouring up.
Dancer's dance-ing. Swishers rolling up
     These girls deep-a piece for all of us.
Strip club bandits-Freak-y in her pumps.
     I can't stand it. Feel-ing on her rump.
The V.I.P's not big enough for us.

PRE-HOOK: (REPEAT TWICE)

CHORUS:

     Girl-whatchu doin' on my lap? She's bouncing
Turn around and bring it back.
     She's teasing-letting you know she's needing stacks.
     She bounce (bounce), bounce. She's dance-ing on my lap.

PRE-HOOK: **(108)**

VERSE II:

     All night long-it's only in the "A."
Strip club naked-drink-ing Chardonnay.
     Got ones and fives-plus stacks is on the way.
Much Ace of Spades-hey-bring another case.
     Three girl's dance-ing popping in my face.
Got money fall-ing. Piles up in the place.
     She all on me-damn it's getting late.
Shame-we claim-this lifestyle-everyday.

REPEAT CHORUS UNTIL MUSIC FADES OUT.

SLOW

HOW COME

VERSE I:

    Baby... does he do you right? Cause you look like... you just had a fight.
    What you cry for... every night? You don't need that... in your life.
    When he hurt you... it always seem-that you fall back... to the same routine.
    If you let me... have a chance to please... I'll provide you... with all you need.

BRIDGE/PRE-HOOK: **(109)**

    Sister... babay... heart-broke... la-day... Need of... hold-ing... squeeze-ing... late-lay.
    Sister... babay... heart-broke... la-day... Need of... hold-ing... squeeze-ing... late-lay.

CHORUS:

    How come... you let... him make... you cry? How come... you take... him back... each time?
    How come... you let-yourself... deny-my love... How come? How come?

VERSE II:

    How long... will you keep take-ing this pain? That he gives you-it's not a game...
    I can grant you... the finer things... that'll lead to... you with my last name...
    Your blind-ed... by cupids sling... and you fall-ing. Can I spread my wings?
    Oh darling... better things... await you. Will you ride with me.

BRIDGE/PRE-HOOK:

REPEAT CHORUS UNTIL MUSIC FADES OUT.

MID TEMPO

I LOVE THE STREETS

VERSE I:

We go way back... when the jack for the sign on the Cadillac.
Get a chain then we hang it around our neck.
In the hood we all good buying food with stamps.
When we all get together.
The little shack-with the lady that was crazy-we threw rocks at.
Got older now we take her some groceries back.
Reminisce about the whole neighborhood on crack
....hey...

CHORUS: (REPEAT TWICE)

I love the streets... I want the whole world to know.
So I run the streets... Stay-ing always on the go.
I love the streets... I survived on my own.
So I run the streets-the streets is where I am from.

VERSE II: (110)

My Auntie Pat-lost a son who fell victim to circumstance.
Ham gone-peaceful journey-now bring it back.
Peanut butter with no jelly that's all we had (in the ghetto).
They're drink-ing Jack-the homeless man and the corner.
The strippers act-like they're famous who can blame'em.
The bootleg maxed. Get-ing money-social service and shooting craps.

REPEAT CHORUS UNTIL MUSIC FADES OUT.

UP TEMPO

SOON OR A LATER

VERSE I:

       I need to see what's up-cause she is fly.
Body like an hour glass-she should be mine.
       Georgio Armani shades-the scene is right.
Popping champagne-no thang. My game is tight.
       Soon as she looks this way- a green light.
I got my swagger on-and it be like...
       Gucci on my proper frame... fitting just right.
Diamonds all up in my chain-and she like.

BRIDGE/PRE-HOOK

       Soon (soon), soon or a later-I will be roll-ing with you. Soon (soon), soon or a later-I'm going home with you.
       Soon (soon), soon or a late-we're going to do what we're spose to. Soon (soon), soon or a later-we're gonna make the big move.

CHORUS: (REPEAT TWICE)   (111)

       Soon or a later-you're gonna be mine...
Pop a couple bottles-pour it up anytime.
       Soon or a later-Cupids gonna take flight...
Love in this club-we're rolling out tonight.

VERSE II:

       All I can tell you-that you're gonna be mine.
Balling divine-close your eyes and fantasize.
       Girl-you're amaze-ing-you and I will be nice.
Give me a chance-to send you off to paradise.
       Money and power-luxury clean ice.
Just say the word babe-you ball-ing out with me tonight.
       Buy out the bar-if not it wouldn't be right.
See you and I-cruise-ing Benz and it's off white.

REPEAT CHORUS UNTIL MUSIC FADES OUT.

MID TEMPO

THIS LITTLE SPOT

CHORUS:
      I know a little wall in hole-where no one goes.
Put on some sexy shoes and clothes-show your toes.
      Then we can have a couple drinks-give a toast.
I know this little spot-let's go to this little spot.

VERSE I:
      Hey how you doing girl? Excuse me your body's banging.
Just call me Mr. Real-100 he never faking.
      How can I spoil you-and possibly get you naked?
Naw'll I'm just play-ing lady-can I get to know you maybe?
      Let me in your world-I'll take you to first class.
Love how you lick your lips-you say that I'm moving fast.
      Well let me slow it down-excuse me I'm chasing cash.
I'll show how to slow role-check out my slow role.

CHORUS: (REPEAT TWICE)
VERSE II: **(112)**
      I love how you do it girl-your beauty has caught my eyes.
      Hope I'm not coming to strong-you got me hypnotized.
      I'll take you across the world-sit back enjoy the ride.
      Will you be my girlfriend? You know I'm just play-ing.
      How bout we salsa dance? Martini Club let's romance.
      There's one joint across from Visions. The mood have you holding hand.
      I didn't know loving-until I looked in your eyes.
I'm trying to know you. I wanna know you.

REPEAT CHORUS UNTIL MUSIC FADES OUT.

UP TEMPO

MY COACH BAG

VERSE I:

        Can't wait 'til I feel... the mu-sic...
I hear it's some par...ties go-ing on...
        I'm going to en-joy... myself...
Give a treat to myself....
        And forget all that's going... wrong

BRIDGE/PRE-HOOK

        Let's chill... Fri-day night.
Every-things gonna be al-right
        Let the hard times pass you by.
And put your gear on... get fly-so I...

CHORUS: (REPEAT TWICE)

        Check-my... hair and ... nails my...
Coach-Bag... com-pli-ment-my plat-form sandals.
        Now I'-fly-ing... soar-ing high-and
Scoop my girls we-club with style-and...

VERSE II: (113)

        Louis V... Christian D...
Tip the d.j.. drinks on me...
        On our way... 2 V.I.P...
Get our dance on... All night yes I...

BRIDGE/PRE-HOOK

REPEAT CHORUS TWICE:

MID-TEMPO
IN FOR THE NIGHT

VERSE I:
    I think all that I need... just you and me baby...
Let's just watch a movie-cuddle on me lady...
    We can stay until three... everything is gravy...
Ignore the phone if it rings... tonight will be a-maze-ing...
    After long we'll be gone... love-ing each other.
All on each other.
    Make-ing love in the sheets... under the covers...
(under the co-vers)
    It's been a while so we need... Time with each other...
    (under each other)
You're so precious to me... You are my lover...
    (you are my lover)

CHORUS: (REPEAT CHORUS TWICE)   (114)
    Tell your girls-you'll be... alright.
Have a ball-no bars...
    We're in for the night...
We're in... we're in... for the... night. We're in...
    We're in... for... the... night.

VERSE II:
    You're my one and only... Loving you like crazy....
I think for life we're going to be... with each other (baby)...
    Check my heart when it beats... For you lucky lady... Im not worried about the streets... As long as you're here baby...

OUTRO:
    Been alone it get's deep...fall-ing in further... for one another...
    Ignore the door... let them beat... cause I'm all on you... loving all on you.
    It's been awhile so we need
time with each other... time with each other...
    You're so precious to me...
    You are my lover... you are my lover...

MID

SO SNEAKY

CHORUS:

      She's so-sneak...y (she's so-sneak...y)
She's so-freak...y (she's so-freak...y)
      She's so-sneak...y (she's so-sneak...y)
She's so sneak...y (she's so-freak...y)

VERSE I:

      This had to be.... The biggest scheme...
in history... For centuries...
      She lied to me... She cried to me...
Confuse-ing me... Use-ing me...
      I bought her thins... And gave her keys...
To all my fleets... And all my cheese...
      The girl-get's down... She creeps around...
Constantly-everyone knows...but me...

CHORUS: (REPEAT TWICE) (115)

VERSE II:

      This girl so fine... She got my mind...
on ho-micide... su-icide...
      She got me blind... Don't know what kind...
of love we got... I'm tore up...
      Here game is tight... She stalks the night...
Vampire bite... Sexy eyes...
      She likes the fame... She got me drained...
Can I be saved... from her fangs..?

MID

P.O.E

CHORUS:

      I'm poe... Chopping down blocks to get my-dough.... Cause I'm a product of environment.
      P.O.E. Bagging up green to get my cheese... Cause I'm a product of environment.

VERSE I:

      Oh! Big Foe zone flippa... yo!
Money ain't a thang now... go.
      Whip game supa' proper... oh!
Weed, speed, trees, boy, and... blow.
      Hustle all day, night and... morn'.
The project still the same got... dough.
      Check my Gucci frames-stunt some...
Mo' everything is everything.

CHORUS: (REPEAT TWICE)   **(116)**

VERSE II:

      Smoke-mean Joe Green-puffing dro.
Wait-ing on my thing to ring... so...
      Run down to the mall-cope some- clothes.
Dead freah everything... dope.
      Hope up in my whip-and I... coast.
Twenty-east never go-ing broke.
      Back up in the trap-cook some mo'.
A million dollars on the way.

REPEAT CHORUS UNTIL MUSIC FADES OUT.

UP TEMPO

DADDY'S ANGEL

CHORUS:

      I'm dad-dy's an-gel (an-gel)...
My dad-dy's little (an-gel)...
      Spread my wings-like God's An-gel.
So I sing-I sing like An-an-gels.

VERSE I:

      This go out to the daddy's...
Standing tall through the storm...
      Thank God that he had me...
And your love kept me warm...
      Without you what would I do?
Cause of you mama fun...
      Make you proud what I do.
To the world make it known.

BRIDGE: (117)

      Like clouds up above...
Cloud nine with my daddy.
      And he been showing love...
I love my daddy...

CHORUS: (TWICE)

      Ain't a card that can picture this....
It ain't a big enough store...
      When he's gon' like where daddy went?
Full of smiles from the door...
      I look just like you...
Will you take me to the store.?
      Loving my daddy he's so cool...
and me he adores.

"DEDICATED TO JORDYN WILSON"

POP

SLUMBER PARTY

CHORUS:

       I'm (I'm) having a slum-ber par-ty...
And I'm gonna tell every-body...
       In-vite all of my friends-just watch me...
Fun (fun) dance-ing around my par-ty...

VERSE I:

       You-know just-how the par-ty goes...
Me-and-all my friends-pajama jams in clothes...
       Li-sten to mu-sic fast or slow....
Dance like we're in the videos...
       Snack-ing while watch-ing mo-vies...
Gossiping as the night goes on...
       Candy Crush theme we foolin'...
It's a celebration all night long.

REPEAT CHORUS TWICE: (118)

VERSE II:

       Tonight we run loose with no control...
The girls get-ting loud... we run the show...
       A whole lot of fun-an overdose...
Joy to the world... let's give a toast...
       Nothing can kill my spirit...
I'm so excited bout to blow...
       The music is loud-you hear it..?
Spin-ing around-till we explode...

REPEAT CHORUS UNTIL MUSIC FADES OUT.

POP

A PARTY THIS WEEKEND

CHORUS:
        No school after this evening...
I can't wait to party this weekend...
        We deserve a two-day vacation...
T.G.I.F. yes it's the weekend...

VERSE I:
        I'm so bored I can barely stay up...
A kid just took the hall pass-I'm out of luck...
        Can't wait till three o'clock-I had enough...
I gotta pay attention don't wanna flunk...
        You stay here then-it's the weekend...
I got some plans-when I leave class...
        Fun and- games and- lot's of sleep-ing...
Need one rea-son... to miss school...

CHORUS: (REPEAT TWICE)   **(119)**

VERSE II: SHANIAH JONES TYPE SONG

        The teacher keeps pacing between us...
I'm feel-ing very la-zy... I just ate my lunch...
        I hope there's a holiday-in there-this month...
I need a break-this school work is way too tough...
        A vaction... or spring break-ing...
Steady wait-ing... cele-brate-ing...
        Re-creation... lot's of play-ing...
Cut the chase-ing... no rules...

OUTRO:
        No school (no school)... week-end with no rules...
No school (no school)... Week-ends are so cool...
        No school (no school)... week-end with no rules...
No school (no school)... weekends are so cool...

MID TEMPO

GIVING YOUR HEART BACK

CHORUS:

   I'm giving your heart back... so I won't... waste your time...
I'm giving your heart back... so I won't... waste your time...
   I'm giving your heart back... no more... you and I...
I'm giving your heart back... so long... girl good-bye.

VERSE I:

   I'll always love you and I mean it...
Fiending for you please believe it...
   Causing hurt is not meant for me...
Before I do I rather leave...
   I wrote you a letter-you didn't read it...
I need some time-to train my feel-ings...
   All these girls surrounding me-I know would kill you-If I cheat...

CHORUS: (REPEAT TWICE)   (120)

VERSE II:

   I know you love me... who can't see it...
But it's many-different reasons...
   Point-ing for my heart to lead...
In directions-tempt-ing me...
   Don't want to be weak-and have you heated...
Feel-ings towards me-scorn and steam...
   You're the best that I can see...
But there's some-thing else I need....

REPEAT CHORUS UNTIL MUSIC FADES OUT.

POP

LAST CALL

INTRO:

        Last (last)- Call (call) for alcohol.
They're call-ing last (last)- Call (call) to party ya'll.

VERSE I:

        She knows she got it m-ade...
She's gonna dance the whole night a-way...
        Girls all up on the stage...
Party all night-in a rave...
        The mu-sic system bang...
To a whole other type of bass...
        Hey D.J. let it play...
Gonna keep on til I hear him say...

CHORUS:

        Last call for alcohol... last call (last call)...
Last call to get your par-ty on...
        Last call to move your body...
You ain't gotta go home but you got to be gone...

VERSE II: (121)

        Just let the record play...
We're going hard until the music fades...
        I smell the purple haze...
Soar-ing it got me in a daze...
        The party's in this place...
Floor is jam packed-people in a craze...
        Beat bump can you hear the bass..?
Get your hands up... till we hear them say...

REPEAT CHORUS UNTIL MUSIC FADES OUT.

SLOW TEMPO

CHARM

INTRO:
    Go ahead and work that thing on me...
Wave that wand girl-work that thing...

CHORUS:
    Girl you have the charm (charm), charm...Working like a wand (wand), wand...
    Make me want to come spend ones...At another show-for another show...
    Girl you have the charm (charm), charm...Where in the world did you come from..?
    I'm throwing out all-my-ones...At another show (at another show)...

VERSE I:
    Girl you work that pole...When you do it slow.
Make me want some more...Need another show.
    Move your booty slow...Round and round, it goes.
    Girl I wanna know...How long you will go.

BRIDGE: **(122)**
    I can see you home with me...A real big house-and family...
 I want to buy you everything...I'll save you-you just dance for me...
    I can see you love-ing me...In the bed-just come with me...
I wanna give you everything...I'll save you just-dance for me...

CHORUS (REPEAT TWICE)

VERSE II:
    Just so that you know-you can have the dough.
But before you go-drop it to the floor.
    Pause it when you stroll-do that sexy pose.
Please don't get me wrong-I love with no clothes.

POP

HEY BARTENDER

BRIDGE:
      Conjur. Nuvo. Armandale. I need another drink (drink).
Vodka. Cognac. Champagne. Pass another drink (drink).

CHORUS:
      Hey bartender-showing love on the drinks drinks).
Stacks on full-my cup is on "E" ("E").
      V.I.P. crowded-I need another drink (drink).
Hey bartender fix me up a drink (drink).

VERSE I:
      Sounds... bump-ing-Drinks... pour-ing.
Slow... motion. Crowd...-dancing (dancing).
      Blowed... Smoking. Throwed... drunken (drunken).
Cold... blooded. She... Hustling (hustling).
      Drinks... coming-beat... running (running).
Keep... goin. Keep... flowing (flowing).
      He's... wasted. Beat... Banging (banging).
No... chasing. Hands... raising (raising).

BRIDGE: (REPEAT TWICE)   **(123)**

CHORUS:

VERSE II:
      Oh..! baby- So...fade-ed (fade-ed).
Four... Aces. Yac... ancient (ancient).
      Crowd... raveing...Cups waving (waving).
Heat... making. Drinks... kick in (kick in).
      Girls... tripping. Keep spilling' (spilling).
Bartender...We're tipping (tipping).
      Good... living. We're winning (winning).
Stilll ... spending. Keep... balling (balling).

MID-TEMPO

HIGH SCORE

INTRO/BRIDGE
    You got me high (high.
You got the high score.
    You got me high (high).
You got the high score.

CHORUS:
    You got a smile… all the girls dream for…
And a style… that can only be yours…
    The way you dance… Make me wanna see more…
You changed the game… you got the high score.

VERSE I:
    The way she drop from the back.
Makes me want to stack.
    Make it clap for dollar.
She's scrubbing the floor (floor).
    Ace of spades. Bottles pour. In the air.
Smoke soars.
    Her smile her style….
Got me throwing out more…

(124)

CHORUS:

VERSE II:
    She's the best. Check the stats. Nicki Minaj from the back.
    All the other girls hawking. They're hating on yours (yours).
    She's got eyes like a cat. Sexy thighs in them stacks.
    You had the joint bumping-since you stepped in the door.

BRIDGE/PREHOOK: (REPEAT TWICE)

REPEAT CHORUS UNTIL MUSIC FADES OUT.

MID-TEMPO

TO BE BOSS

VERSE I:
        Beating down the block-you know just how we do it.
Check my trap spots-throw up the deuces-keep it moving.
        Money in my socks-all up in my pockets.
I know the feds watch-I'm a ball until they stop it.
        I'm going to call the shots and add up all the profit.
Gucci and Vutton-blessed wit street knowledge.
        I'm back from a loss (ooh)! Now I'm back on (hmmm)
And the throne-will be mine now on…

CHORUS:
        All the diamonds I got… necklace and my wrist watch.
Cars parked up the block… Girls in different flocks.
        (What it means to be boss)
        Now invest-in stock… Flossing gator blocks.
Bread fold in knots… I'm soaring to the top.
        (What it means to be boss)

VERSE II: **(125)**

        It's nothing to be the boss-The life I chose-and used it.
Ain't worried bout the cops… I'm making lit music.
        They want my soul to rott…but they ain't got the heart to do it.
I'm flying pass them all… while the hater's keep losing.
        Saluting to my mob… the ones I feel the truest.
Time to be smart… fed the Brain, now use it.
        lights flash on… (mmm!) Stunting shades on, (yeah!)
And I feel-it's my time so strong.

MID

WIT' MY HEAD

VERSE I:
    Tugging on my heart-you got me on one...
You're not supposed to be here-where did you come from?
    I had to many drinks-this is my last one...
Bring that m thing closer-let me cut some...
    I wanna wake up to you-everyday...
I'm fiend-ing inside-keep dancing that way...
    You're bouncing that thing on me...
Your body is calling me...

CHORUS:
    The way she move it and drop it it's messing wit my head.
The way she shake it and pop it, her booty calling me.
    Baby teasing me-freaking me-lingerie in all red.
Tell me why it seems she's playing.

BRIDGE/PRE-HOOK:
    (126)

    Wit my head (wit my head)-WIt my head (wit my head)
Wit my head (wit my head)-Wit my head (wit my head)

VERSE II:
    Girl the way you've been grind-ing on me all night...
    Make me feel special-just you and I. lost in these feelings-I'm spose to hide...
    I wonder do you feel the same girl..? See the way... you look in my eyes...
    Seems like you want me inside... I wonder if I should just try...
    Give me a lap... dance, please!

CHORUS:

REPEAT CHORUS UNTIL MUSIC FADES OUT.

UP TEMPO

DESIGNER SHADES

INTRO/BRIDGE:

      Girls get mad when they see how you do it.
Fly chick-bad make it do what it do.

VERSE I:
      Excuse me hey-The way you rocking those shades...
Them Cartiers?
      Them Fox Brown-gold trimmed-looking frames.
You set-stakes high-slim what's you r name?
      Your mood smooth-like your body move.
Ray Ban shades
      The way you're copping them specs...
I copped them Jay's...
      I just bought a new six like yesterday...
You're style sleek like silk (silk) lingerie...
      (and I'm trying to get in...)

CHORUS: (REPEAT TWICE)
      She's up on game-the girl wear-ing designer shades.
      Check the name-on the right side of the frames.
Bet it say-class in all kind of ways-
      Fit her face shape-all day everyday.

VERSE II: **(127)**
      Armani shades-or the Gucci it'll do it.
With matching shoes all on you.
      Baby girl so cute-she like to flip it all kind of colors.
Powder-blue. Make it do what it do.
      Girls envy you-dark tint on the Prada glasses.
Coogi shoes. Small hips with a lot of ass, dimples too.
      She has bank rolls-hella cash-Louie boots.
I guess it's all on you.

REPEAT CHORUS UNTIL MUSIC FADES OUT.

MID TEMPO

GIRL YOU THE FINEST

VERSE I:
　　　　Girl your body's hot in the right spots.
Bring your benz on off in my chop shop.
　　　I go hard-and trust me wont stop.
Don't hold back-no neighbors for six blocks.
　　　　Climb all up the walls-to the tip top.
Girl you that thang to me.

BRIDGE/PRE-HOOK:
　　　I can't help the fact that I'm fiending.
Probably cause your back side the reason.
　　　　Got your hair and nails down this evening.
Peaches and cream with expensive weave in.

CHORUS: **(128)**
　　　I like the way you walk-got a figga stuck-
Cant' even talk-you got me fiending.
　　　　Girl you the finest. (finest and you shining).
Girl you the finest-shine like a diamond…
　　　　Lip gloss-pouty mouth-that booty round. Must be the South-I'm fiending.
　　　　Girl you the finest-(fine and you shining).
Girl you the finest-shine like white diamonds.

Chris Brown Type Song

VERSE II:
　　　　Loud and drank-you got the boys leaning.
Pull on up-you hear the trunk beating.
　　　Let me spoil-you for the evening. I am what your
body been needing.
　　　　From way back you caught the boy peeping.
I can't front-off my feet you're sweeping.
　　　Let's do lunch-plenty eating.
I got bread-and I'll do the treating.

REPEAT CHORUS UNTIL MUSIC FADES OUT.

SLOW

GOT ME GOSSIPING

VERSE I:

       I told my girl today is your birthday...
and they play these games-call me your name...
       We gossip back in forth in the best way...
and I tell some things-without shame.
       And my heart won't change...
unles something strange...
       something strange come over me...
without you I promise-there is no me...
       It's just mutual understanding...
loving you-loving me.

CHORUS: (REPEAT TWICE)   (129)

       The way you love me and...
Never mistreat me when...
       I go out with my friends...
you got me gossipin'.
       All of the time we spend...
Holding eachother when...
       I'm shopping with my friends...
I get's to gossipin'.

VERSE II:

       Just being a part of you is a blessing...
we started out as friends-I hope it never ends...
       Some times love and fate is the question...
Guess it all depends... who the person is...
       All of my girls-say they see the change in me.
It's a glow you shine down on me...
       And I appreciate the way you-brought that on me.
I guess it's mutual understanding-loving you loving me.

CHORUS: (REPEAT TWICE)

SLOW

CHOCOLATE CAKE

VERSE I:

   It's four in the morn-ing...
Some-one's knocking at my door...
   She say-she's been yearning...
For what she had-the night before...
   We all-lost in the mo-ment...
Stir it fast and-stir it slow...
   She like's-how I'm-serve-in...
It's so sweet-she want some more...

CHORUS: (REPEAT TWICE)

   Choc-late cake... I give her that choc-late cake...
needing that-choc-late cake... (filled with that love inside)...
   Cho-clate cake... She's wanting that...
chocolate cake...
   I feed her that choc-late cake-(filled with that love in-side).

VERSE II: (130)

   I wan-na know... if-you like choc-late...
Reddish brown-dou-ble fudge... dark choc-late...
   Eat-it up... I'm sure... you'll love it...
All-the time... rich and fine... in your sto-mach...

BRIDGE: (REPEAT TWICE)

   Go ahead-have a piece...
Go ahead-have a piece...
   Slow it down...it's your piece...
Slow it down-it's your treat...

REPEAT CHORUS UNTIL MUSIC FADES OUT.

"While going through some of the roughest times in my life, I often turned to writing. Writing was therapy for me. It was an outlet to free my mind. At any given time I was able close my eyes and write about everything floating through my mind. I mostly wrote music and song lyrics as well as movie scripts and screenplays.

Throughout my years in entertainment I spent countless hours in studio recording sessions. During those times, in my opinion, I realized one of the main time consuming issues in a recording session is the artist taking too long to write, or not being able to come up with fresh content, lyrics or ideas to record at all. Let's face it. STUDIO TIME IS EXPENSIVE!

I provided these song and timeless lyrics so that aspiring singers and songwriters who write or don't write have a collection of songs to record a demo album to, so that they can display their talents to record companies, music producers, or even just to friends and family.

These songs were published for promotional use only. With a purchase order or receipt from this book download, the artist can record any of these songs to complete their demo album.